The Boys at the Bar

The Boys at the Bar

Antics of a Vanishing Breed of Cowboys & Hellions

SUREVA TOWLER

Johnson Books

BOULDER

For Rachel, Regan, and Sadie Mae Keller

*To encourage them to slay dragons, drink red beer,
dance on tabletops, and pee in the woods,
not necessarily in that order*

Published by Johnson Books, a division of Big Earth Publishing,
3005 Center Green Drive, Suite 220, Boulder, Colorado 80301.
E-mail: books@bigearthpublishing.com
www.johnsonbooks.com

Cover photo: Down at the Corral Club, where Old Robert Nefzger more often
than not rides in to end the day with a couple or three beers, his mare Congo
waits patiently out back until closing time. Fearing for Bob's safety on the return
trip, the Boys at the Bar rigged the horse out with "tail lights." Photo by Dee
Richards

Cover design: Constance Bollen, cbgraphics
Composition by Eric Christensen

9 8 7 6 5 4 3 2 1

Library of Congress Cataloging-in-Publication Data
Towler, Sureva.
    The boys at the bar: antics of a vanishing breed of cowboys & hellions / Sureva Towler.
        p. cm.
    ISBN 1-55566-377-X
    1. West (U.S.)—Humor. 2. City and town life—Humor. I. Title.
    PN6231.W4T69 2006
    814'.6—dc22   2006004141

Printed in the United States of America

Contents

Acknowledgments ix

Introduction
The Boys at the Bar 3

On Change
Geography of Love 9
Altitude Spawns Attitude 11
The Changing West 14
No Place Like Home 16
Landscaping the West 18
The Architecture of Change 21
Growing Cash on the Back Forty 23

On Rocky Mountain Couth
Colorado Dreaming 29
Colorado Roadtrips 31
Colorado Chic 33
Colorado Romance 35
Colorado Winters 38
Colorado Pack Rats 40
Colorado Matchmaking 43

On Cowboys
Eulogy for a Cowboy 47
Their Lifestyle 49
Their Virtues and Vices 51
Their Design 53
Their Poetry 56
Their Horses 58
Their Garages 60

On Community

Paying Your Dues........................65
School Bonds...........................67
Culture Mavens........................69
Budget Busters.........................71
Book Clubs............................73
Potluck Suppers........................75
Planners..............................77
Life in Eventsville......................79

On Holidays

Granny's Commencement Address...........85
Granny's Marriage Counseling.............87
Opening Day...........................89
Kansas Is for the Birds...................91
Thanksgiving Ain't for Turkeys 93
Cowboy Christmas......................95
Getting Ready for the New Year............97

On Cuisine

Hunting Camp Gourmet.................103
Cowboy Caviar 105
Cowboy Appetizers 107
Coffee in a Tin Cup....................109
Sara Lee Is My Best Friend 111

On Pals

Girlfriends 117
Chuck-the-Hero 119
Crazydave-the-Plumber 121
Glen-the-Fisherman 124
Carla-the-Soccer-Mom 126
Laurie-the-Hairdresser 128
Nancy-the-Collector 129
Maude-the-Widow-Woman 131
Millie-the-Life-Coach 134
Gert-the-Extension-Agent 136
Mindi-the-Homeless-Rich-Homeowner 138
Wanda-Jane-the-Hellion 140

The Old West had been settled by dreamers, great-hearted adventurers who were impractical to the point of magnificence; a courteous brotherhood, strong in attack but weak in defense, who could conquer but could not hold. Now all the vast territory they had won was to be at the mercy of men who had never dared anything, never risked anything. ... The space, the colour, the princely carelessness of the pioneer they would destroy and cut up into profitable bits, as the match factory splinters the Primeval forest.

—Willa Cather, *A Lost Lady*

Acknowledgments

THIS BOOK WAS molded by love, laughter, and Beaujolais nouveau provided by Mike and Maureen Hogue of Routt County's Three Quarter Circles Ranch, Jay Kittleson and Becky Rold of Denver's Vine Street Manor, and the parents of my grandchildren, Tim and Judy Keller of Lawrence, Kansas. Many of these pieces were written for the *Denver Post*, where feature editors Judith Howard and Linda Castrone never permitted me to louse up a good story with bad spelling. I am also grateful to Joanne Palmer for constantly reminding me to "shut up and write," and to Stephanie Reineke and Lori Bourgeois, who let me do it at Geeks Garage in Steamboat Springs, Colorado.

My life has been enriched by the cowboys and carpenters, hoods and hoodlums, who have shared their stories, and by the girlfriends who have listened to me whine about them, particularly Sue Schneller, Chris Ensworth, Carla Mumm, Sheri Lu Steiner, Meg Bentley, Noreen Moore, and Irene Nelson. I am fortunate to live in Steamboat Springs, a rural community that has always insisted that it doesn't want to be like Aspen or Vail, although there is not the slightest possibility that it could be. I am really quite lucky to have endured so much fun with the Boys at the Bar, who know that you can live, love, and laugh hard—but that it will probably kill you.

Introduction

The Boys at the Bar

AT THE HEART of every town in the American West is a neighborhood bar. The Corral Club, Oasis, Antler's, Elks, or Cattlemen's. It doesn't matter whether it's called the Mangy Moose, Lost Dog, or Old Style; it makes a statement about place. It is home for plowjockeys, nailjockeys, slatrats, ranchers, miners, government dumbasses, quick-buck artists, hired men, three-piece suits, Bible-bangers, and drifters.

In my town, the main watering hole sits on the main drag. When it was built in 1954 everyone said it was too far east of town. They were wrong. Everyone said the garbage man was going to be elected Man of the Year. They were right. The Corral Club is where the Good Ol' Boys begin the day drinking coffee and end it with a couple or three beers. It's where Stomps and Freaks get along. Where attitude isn't a problem, it's a way of life. Where you don't have to be rich, beautiful, or halfway smart. You just know not to order a martini.

The seats are covered with cracked maroon Naugahyde. The grease trap has never been cleaned. Everyone knows who put a bullet through the neon sign in front, and no one will tell who stole the sign in back warning, "No Horses Allowed in Bar." Today's "special" will always be chicken-fried steak, mashers, and Jell-O salad—more'n likely with marshmallows. Ketchup and mustard come in squeeze bottles. They keep Schlitz in the cooler for Billy because he's the only guy in town who drinks it, and every now and again Mary Kay tends bar in a nun's habit. The Church Ladies bring their own coffeecake so they won't have to tip the waitress. While wheeler-dealers scribble numbers on napkins, ownership shifts with every game of Bar Booth.

After any noteworthy event—be it rodeo, softball, funeral, or wedding—everyone shows up to pull on a cold one. Perley says no horses are allowed in the place because no one wants to see a long face; but Old Bob Nefzger, who ranched a few miles west of town, rode his mare, Congo, in pretty regular. Locals wear Carharts, refer

3

to their wives as the "Old Lady," smoke, chew, and spit. Wannabees wear logo jeans and cowboy hats with snakeskin bands and feathers. It makes no nevermind who buys the next round because someone always slaps a twenty-dollar bill on the bar. Everyone drinks till it's gone and the guy on the next stool antes up another twenty.

The Corral Club is the hub of social, economic, and political activity. It's where the "regulars" share laughter, lies, and hijinks, tell it like it was, or spin it like they want it to be. It defines who we really are. Nowhere is that better demonstrated than by who goes and who does not, where they sit, how long they stay, and who they go home with. Like every corner pub, it has been responsible for a lot of marriages and even more divorces.

The neighborhood bar is where news is made, shared, and revised. Where stories are told the way you want them remembered, and prizes are awarded for the first, the most, and the biggest, whether a fish, an elk, or a woman. Where tales about your dog, your horse, and your gun get magnified. But no one would dream of pointing out that it really didn't happen that way or that you've told that one seventeen times. On a good day, the Old Lady will call to remind you to come home, other days she just locks you out of the house.

The Boys at the Bar don't give a rat's ass about O.J. or Hillary. They care about the who, where, why, what, and how of real life: who set the fire in the Dumpster behind the garage; where the bowling league stands in the playoffs; why County Road 57 isn't paved; what the commissioners plan to do about the gravel pit; how the Beavers, Badgers, or Bears will redeem themselves Friday night.

While the latest Blue Ribbon Committee is huddled in the basement of the elementary school "visioning" what the quality of life in the community should be, the Boys at the Bar can tell you. They don't need a Power Point presentation, a 12-step program, a facilitator, or a planning director to examine the meaning of life. They know when the bond issue is going down, whether the super-intendent of schools needs to be replaced, and which city council-man is green-belting his property. They are equal parts nosey old ladies and bona fide historians.

They remember the preacher's daughter who danced on tabletops when she was feeling sassy; the interior decorator who drove into town with four kids in a bread truck; the gal who won the wet T-shirt contest back before she was elected to city council; the guy who traded his 40-year-old wife in for two 20s. They're still chuckling about the night Pat drank on the roof because someone said "drinks were on the house"; the afternoon Sam's horse ate the lettuce off Lena's hamburger; and the time Darwin stole the Greyhound bus while the driver was having coffee at the Harbor Hotel.

After a few beers, the props to implement some sort of caper always seem to be at hand. Anything goes as long as you endanger no life but your own and you come home with a good story, preferably on yourself. Raiders fans are required to cover their heads with bags during Bronco games, and everyone leaves their pickups running so they'll be warm at closing time. The Corral Club is where the Code of the West was invented, interpreted, and enforced.

It does not exist in the past; it's a symbol of the present. The Code of the West has adapted to building and sign codes, the demands of handicapped access and health inspections, but it has not changed. The waitresses will always be named Ida, Agnes, or Betty Jean, and will generally be underage. The patrons will always be Shorty, Slim, Tex, and Red. The guys with big hats and no cattle drink elbow-to-the-bar with bricklayers. The mayor has his own key. The only reason to leave the bar is to attend the National Western Stock Show in Denver. And being 86'd is the end of the road: worse than losing your saddle, having to shoot your horse, or taking a bath. Or as Mike sez, "I'd rather be caught with someone else's wife."

On Change

Geography of Love

We met at the Corral Club, where he was shooting pool and I was drinking a martini. The Boys at the Bar said the marriage would never last.

He came from the oil fields in Wyoming's Teapot Dome country and spent his summers in the Big Horn Mountains. I came from the National Cathedral School for Girls and summered on a gentlemen's farm on the eastern shore. He was raised in a trailer by his grandpa, an oiler in Wyoming's Salt Creek Flats. I grew up in the burbs with a cook and a chauffeur. I was a member of the Choir of Angels. He ran sheep for his Uncle Harry.

I was, as my father was so fond of pointing out, "to the manor born." Crazydave was born knowing how to shoot pool and a .22. He was never a pro at school. He learned to read off the back of a cereal box, got lousy grades in citizenship, and was destined for academic oblivion, until he fell in love with the sharpest chick in fifth grade. By eighth grade he had accumulated certificates and letters for sports, attendance, Little League, sharpshooting, and reporting for the school paper.

He attended Sterling Junior College, where he chaired the Drawers Corps, a bunch of hellions who majored in acquiring trophies from girls' dorms. I studied English at New York University. He mended fence and worked with his hands. I read e.e. cummings and hadn't a clue what I was going to do with my life. He used an outhouse until he was sixteen. I had never seen one. I used Hollandaise. He used ketchup.

He found trouble by stealing the family car, mastering the art of pushing it out of the driveway and down the block before starting the engine. I got caught stuffing a mailbox full of leaves, getting nabbed by a neighbor who claimed to be a *Life* magazine reporter, working, as fate would have it, on a story about why girls from nice families fall into lives of crime.

We both grew up violating the bedtime hour by reading under the covers with a flashlight. Lone Ranger for him, Nancy Drew for me.

Not too dissimilar when you think about it. Tonto always had his ear to the ground trying to figure out which way the horses went, and Nancy was forever crawling through cobwebs trying to find out whodunit. Like them, and like everyone who went West or grew up in the West, we wanted to be mavericks.

The West was big enough for all of my dreams and all of his antics. Love creates its own geography. We never leave home without jumper cables, and we don't like seeing the American flag used for shirts or underpants. We know whose kids are going to get nailed for poaching or speeding. We read the police blotter, use "fuzz busters," and have seen the inside of the county slammer.

I accept the fact that it's bad luck to take women to hunting camp, and he knows it's bad manners to wear a hat in the house. We don't buy our clothes at Lands' End, and we have little use for people in black spandex pants and helmets with rearview mirrors. He doesn't respect anyone who hasn't fallen off a bull at least once, and I don't trust anyone who doesn't like to fish. He doesn't visit his mother, and I don't go to doctors. It's the Code of our West.

Crazydave is intensely involved with who wins which football game, and I don't make Jell-O salad or Divinity. His heroes are Charlie Goodnight and Robert Redford; mine are Eleanor Roosevelt and Hillary Clinton. He likes Discovery Channel, I watch CNN. He can get lost in James Michener and not return to work until a book is finished. And although I get credit for the fact that, between annual trips to the Central City Opera, the house rocks with Pavarotti, I would rather be listening to George Jones. We've agreed not to learn to line dance, but we may never reach consensus on whether Wal-Mart or the wolf has caused more damage in the land.

Today's Westerners are singers, truck drivers, athletes, artists, and drywallers. Very few ride rodeo and even fewer are related to cows. They sing, drink, dance, and write godawful poetry. They are supposed to be sustained by the smell of hay and manure. They're supposed to be great liars and lovers. But, even if more of us are naming our daughters Abby and Emma, I've yet to see anyone stir frijoles with the barrel of a Colt.

Condos have displaced cows, cell phones have replaced party lines, and Starbucks draws bigger crowds than supper in the church basement. But bottom line: Guys who like hot sauce and run for the REA Board don't have too much trouble getting lucky.

On our twenty-fifth anniversary Crazydave-the-Plumber gave me a .30-30 because, he said, that's how the West was won. I gave him a black satin nightie because, I said, that's how everything is won.

The Boys at the Bar were wrong.

Altitude Spawns Attitude

SOMETHING STRANGE HAPPENS to people who live above 10,000 feet and drink water from icy mountain streams. They know that life is a do-it-yourself event and that it requires you to show up and be the hero of your own story. They know how to survive three-wire-winters and how to defrost pipes, jury-rig electricity, and jump-start old trucks. They can fix anything with rope and baling wire.

They know the difference between an ass and a donkey, a park and a meadow, a blowdown and a blowout. They work hard and play hard, and can drink and laugh while doing both. Pa can keep the baler running fifteen years after it's fully depreciated. Ma can run to town for parts and feed the hay crew while changing diapers. Their kids know how to pull calves, clear ditches, and round up cattle.

In the mountains you learn how to fight because you are always battling weather, poverty, ornery stock, or people who violate fence lines. In the mountains you're too busy surviving to spend time on a shrink's couch or in a confessional. But you're never too busy to tell stories. "In the end, stories are what's left of us," says Salman Rushdie. "We are no more than the few tales that persist." In the world where people hunt and fish to put meat on the table, laughter and lies put our lives in perspective and they remind us of the pressing need to spend life well.

The Boys at the Bar are not dummies. They stay on top of things. They know how to translate rumors, half-truths, and make-believe into stories. Sometimes they change the names to protect the guilty or to preserve marriages, but their tales are all more-or-less true. Their stories are about people who steal outhouses and cheat on building inspectors. They are about the *really* important things in life: hunting camp, the school bond election, the bowling league, and the town council. But mostly they are about change in the West, Brie-eaters moving into the land of American cheese.

To the dismay of the generation that had to cut ice from the river, haul water from the creek, and slop mud from a soddie, the West is changing. Shane left, Old Yeller passed over, and Zane Grey is out of print. The Indians, mountain men, homesteaders, and cowboys have ridden into the sunset, replaced by Cappuccino Cowboys, Tree-huggers, and Eco-devos who rode in on jets.

Everyday life in remote western towns is changing. Dot.com millionaires are buying "ranch experiences" from guys used to riding their horses into bars and being served. Men named Clint and women named Clara are neighboring with newcomers named Carleton and Cassandra. Small-town values are colliding with big-city developers. Ranchers are being forced to choose between profit and preservation. Biscuits and gravy are being replaced by biscotti and ginkgo.

The Boys at the Bar are the *real* endangered species. Ironically, there are support groups for the battered and abused, for illiterates, alcoholics, and people suffering from cancer, chronic fatigue, or grief. But where is the sustenance for aging ranchers, loggers, miners, and welders, who build the legacies we blather about preserving? Their voices and values are disappearing.

Plato said there were seven basic plots. In the Old West they were simple:

(1) When Daddy came over the Pass, the wheel fell off the wagon.

(2) We damn well wudda starved to death if we hadn't eaten Ol' Nell.

(3) Cavalry beat shit out of the Indians.

(4) Cattlemen beat shit out of the sheepmen.

(5) Small town beat shit out of the sheriff.

(6) Bad guy turns preacher.

(7) Soiled dove goes to the laundry.

The New West is far more complicated. Up at Dry Lake you can find cars parked right next to each other with conflicting bumper stickers. One says "Wilderness: Land of No Use," the other promotes "Wilderness: Preserve It for Our Grandchildren." Today's seven basic plots revolve around different issues:

(1) How long *is* a long-range goal?

(2) Will the smoking ban pass?

(3) What is affordable housing?

(4) Do we *need* more open space?

(5) How do you define "quality of life"?

(6) Should the highway bypass town?

(7) What are we going to do about downtown parking?

It takes agri-economists to plot the ramifications of land use, predator control, price incentives, grazing policies, diet fads, foreign trade, and the hole in the ozone layer. The long and the short of it is that there is a world out there, real or imagined, that is dying. It hurts your head and your heart to think about it. Living with it makes you pissy.

"New Westers" are having as much trouble defining change as the Boys at the Bar are having coping with it. Things are not looking good for the Boys at the Bar. They say leafy spurge sure-as-hell will survive, but they're not at all sure about the West.

The Changing West

A THOUSAND ASHLEYS have moved into my town. They all have blonde hair with black roots, acrylic nails, and faux Victorian houses with four-car garages crowned by caretaker apartments. They drive $80,000 Range Rovers and every one of them was born with the right of way. They fight boredom with bridge, and menopause with golf. They read Larry McMurtry and desperately want to get laid by a cowboy.

Their daughters don't know where veal cutlet comes from and their sons think sheep grow fur. Their husbands are Trust Fund Babies who wear ironed jeans and complain about deer stealing vegetables from the garden. They have big bucks and plenty of time to hug trees, spy on birds, and chase elk. They tell us they are the stewards of the land. "Oh wow," they say, "this is way better than Chicago."

They have come to gape at scenic overlooks and play in blue-ribbon trout streams. Our mountains top out at 14,000 feet and a third of the state is public land, so we can host a perfectly splendid Rocky Mountain high. Of course, Mom is already high on Prozac, the kid is zonked on Ritalin, and Dad is busy nurturing the family trusts. To the amusement of the Boys at the Bar, who have saved everything Granddaddy hauled over the Pass in the last hundred years (especially cars), they preach recycling. They are eager to save the environment by turning game trails into nature walks, labeling every shrub and tree in sight, and preserving any rural landscape that doesn't interfere with their plans to build a McCastle on a ridgeline.

At the turn of the last century, my town was so isolated that locals could work off their chamber of commerce dues by shoveling snow off the Pass, allowing visitors to come into town on U.S. 40. The movie house opened when Shorty damn well pleased, and Agnes closed the Corral Club whenever she was ready to go home. If you needed pieces or parts after hours, Doug would trot downtown to open the hardware store, Walt would unlock the gas pump, or Kenny would fill a prescription. They'd spend the whole next day complaining about it, but, hey, what are neighbors for?

Today, charter planes jet in rhinestone cowboys from both coasts. They want to trade flan for fresh air, sauvignon blanc for Coors, Oxfords for Sorrels, and bassets for blue heelers. The Boys at the Bar say it's a really good thing the "new natives" don't have to walk the ditch or run cattle: gives 'em enough time to run around in spandex. Good thing we've got a planning department to gild those thirty-five-acre enclaves. They got here just in time to save us from ourselves and the National Park Service, they say.

Kourtney, "spelled with a K," says she just wants to preserve our lifestyle and catch-and-release fishing. Kourtney owns a snowmobile, a mountain bike, and a kite. She lives in a Gucci subdivision on a spread framed by gigantic gates, no fence. She writes $1,000 checks to the hospital "to prove that she's a good neighbor." She runs for city council "to give something back to the community." Her log house is built from enough trees to shade forty-four acres, and it's decorated with dried cow skulls purchased in Jackson Hole. She spends an inordinate amount of time at cocktail parties discussing how many square feet it contains and how she gets along with her housekeeper.

The Boys at the Bar have no shortage of stories about the last one over the Pass. They're still chuckling about the day Lucille accidentally backed her tractor over the new neighbor's grass while fixing her fence and was asked to repair the damage by tying the grass back up on Popsicle sticks. They remember when the sheriff was called to investigate a complaint about cows being tortured out on Twenty Mile Road only to find that the ranch was branding. They think the Nature Conservancy guys are wizards for running Red Angus on a spread made famous for registering the nation's first Herefords. The Boys at the Bar say God had to put something on this earth dumber than a cow, and they're convinced the last one over the Pass qualifies pretty near every time.

Down at the Corral Club they still relish the good ol' daze: when the librarian stashed a bottle of vodka behind the Britannica; when the couples west of town just up and swapped wives; when the county commissioner pulled a gun on an IRS agent. Life was simpler when road bosses ploughed their friend's driveways and it made no nevermind. Today, the children's librarian is doing cybersex, and the gray-haired lady in reference is arrested for dealing drugs two weeks before the library's bond issue goes to a vote. It's just more than you can handle, even with a shot of Dickel.

The Boys at the Bar shake their heads and wonder at the blonde bombshell skier decked out in suit, gloves, hat, and boots—all yellow. Damn sure has yellow tits, they said. And they chuckle over the hotshot executive's wife who rode into the sunset with the guy who shoed her horses. That was plenty funny because PJ wasn't a very good farrier and everyone knew Bonnie Jean was a lousy lay.

The Boys at the Bar scratch their heads and their crotches and allow as how someone damn well shudda' locked the gate.

No Place Like Home

SINCE OUR FOUNDING FATHER dragged three kids and a cow over the Pass, western Colorado has been hardscrabble country. Settlers have been fighting tough times since 1885, although the country enjoys 72 inches of precipitation and 250 days of sunshine a year. This is good for sheep because the sun bleaches their wool on the hoof, but it's bad for farming because snow limits the growing season to fifty-nine days.

Snow depth is measured by the number of fence wires it covers. A typical three-wire winter involves coping with massive "cabin fever," and four feet of snow slows the pace from November to April. Skiers call it "champagne powder." Developers call it "white gold." The Boys at the Bar call it shit.

Until the highway into town was paved in the '50s, Dry Lake remained an isolated ranching community, equal parts Republican, Democrat, and None-of-Your-Damn-Business. But since a gondola began whisking skiers to the top of the Rockies in the '70s, the population has quadrupled.

Down at the Corral Club they call newcomers "turkeys" and openly discuss how to stiff them. Of course, turkeys are good for the guys who wear nail belts because they build ski lodges bigger'n football fields with Jacuzzis in all seven bathrooms. But the turkeys cannot understand why the town shuts down during hunting season, the plumber is not radio-dispatched, and the electrician reduces his rates if he likes you. I'm here, they say, so we better institute architectural controls and start teaching something besides quilting and stained glass at the community college.

Up at Dry Lake, as in most small towns, locals have always been convinced that whatever was written about the town in marketing brochures was true. They also know what's been left out. The Boys at the Bar know all the details and have, in fact, hoisted a few beers with most of the culprits: The mayor who failed at retail but made a fortune dealing drugs; the substance abuse counselor who was a bona fide alcoholic; the county attorney who doubled as planning director; the social services director who had an affair with a sixteen-year-old girl. Let's face it, once upon a time, the sheriff was a card-carrying member of the Klan, and the county commissioners, on more than one occasion, gave transients a one-way bus ticket out of town.

Several years ago the town adopted a $2 million philosophy: if it didn't cost $2 million, we didn't build it. We built an ice-skating rink from used parts that cost $2 million to repair. We built an addition to the ski lodge that collapsed while under construction and cost $2 million to rebuild. We repaved the main drag the summer before $2 million worth of sewer lines were installed. We built a $2 million bike path with tunnels under the railroad tracks that flood in the spring so local scuba divers don't have to pine for Costa Rica. We built a $2 million airport and before the paint dried, the airline discontinued service, so the terminal is used for community dances.

Somebody paved the road less traveled and diverted the river running through it. The town named the rodeo arena for a real estate salesman instead of the cowboy who built it with Jackpot Rodeo. The greasy spoon was forced to take down its ugly sign. When federal legislation gave us more cops, we assigned them to enforcing leash laws. The chamber of commerce installed a pop machine outside the front door of its new building in violation of codes passed by the beautification committee, and the "hysterical" preservatives slapped a historical marker on a tin barn at the fairgrounds that once housed the county shop.

A city manager was imported from Aspen, the town we most don't want to be like. He moved his desk into the foyer of city hall to "get to know everyone better." Every time the front door opened, the wind swept his desk clean. The Boys at the Bar said he was way smarter than anyone gave him credit for.

Down at the Corral Club, no one is particularly surprised when yet another mega-condo goes belly up or a wife hires a gun to snuff her husband. But when the handsome young couple, so wonderfully active in the PTA, is hauled off for dealing drugs, the chamber ambassadors are totally amazed because, as the chairman continues to point out, "They were such nice people."

Landscaping the West

THERE ARE MORE THAN fifty thousand Master Gardeners in North America, and I am not one of them. In fact, I am convinced that yard work makes you crazy. People who spend too much time with petunias do stupid things. Like the gal down the street whose identity is so tied up in her grassy front yard that she makes her kids wear socks when they play ball. Or the neighbor lady who pops out from behind lace curtains to yell at my dog when he tiptoes across the corner of her lot.

There are incredibly satisfying methods of dealing with these people: collect gone-to-seed dandelion heads and spread them on the lawn as you walk the dog, preferably after midnight. Or splash a little copper sulphate on the meticulously trimmed front hedge as you walk the dog, again, preferably after midnight.

When you live in the West, where thirty-four percent of the land is forest, refuge for wildlife, and national parks and monuments, it's awfully hard to understand why so much time, money, and effort must be devoted to land management. Why must every town with a population over seventeen have pocket parks, greenbelts, open space, and Art in Public Places? Why do people who build houses on ridgelines think they can mitigate the impact by hiring fleets of landscapers, earthmovers, irrigators, stone masons, and urban foresters? How much time can you spend thinking about where to put the pond and how to keep out the deer?

This country boasts more than four thousand environmental groups devoted to conserving nature, preserving wildlife, creating public lands, managing livestock, protecting endangered species, renewing resources, and controlling air, water, and weeds. We have taken over the management of the material world from Mother Nature. But Mother Nature knows that forest fires improve habitat for three-toed woodpeckers, Mexican spotted owls, and northern goshawks. She is fully aware that spring toads shouldn't hang out in Kansas, parsley doesn't flourish in Colorado, and fringed orchids refuse to grow in North Dakota. She planned it this way.

She did it without legislation, treaties, judicial decisions, or regional regulations. And she did it without any help from weed and water control districts. Mother Nature has no degrees in landscaping, environmental sciences, or aesthetics. She wasn't a member of an Audubon Society or nature center. She never attended the annual meeting of a rural electric association, livestock management cooperative, or soil conservation district. In fact, she may have done it in spite of the nature clubbers, bird watchers, and master planners.

What happened to the good ol' daze when we just raised things to eat? Today a new generation of Garden Guerillas is growing medicinal herbs and plants to attract butterflies and hummingbirds. They plant flowers in front of old headboards so they can call 'em flower beds. They golf at Hilton Head, while landscaping lackeys transform the grounds of their starter castles into the Tuileries, and you need a four-wheel golf cart to maneuver their spreads.

Many can't distinguish native grass from weeds, and some are convinced that Rocky Mountain locusts have taken up residence despite the fact that they went extinct in 1908. They cannot be persuaded that fire and wind make forests healthy, or that parsley worms turn into butterflies. They are convinced that insects are malicious, mean, and out to get them. This is not the crowd that grows roses for the county fair.

In the real West, we use horses and pickups to survey our spreads. Garden Gurus, like Gertrude next door, are the size of John Deere tractors and veterans of more than one knee replacement. She wears a straw hat every day except Christmas and has been known to steal trees and harvest seed from national forests.

Up at Dry Lake, we plant hens 'n' chicks in our old galoshes and nail them up by the front door. We can chokecherries, serve coffee that tastes like Roundup, and mostly grow tomatoes for spaghetti sauce. We know that it's soil if it's in the backyard, and dirt if it's on your shirt.

This year we're planning a High Altitude Garden Festival devoted to Weeds of the World. We're going to have prizes for the best weed, the most outstanding yard art, the most unique wind chimes, and the finest use of yard lights. There will be awards for outstanding culverts, trash containers, clotheslines, and wheelbarrows. Prizes will be given for the best, largest, and most creative outdoor grill, and the most imaginative use of door ornaments. Abandoned lawn mowers will be afforded special recognition.

The county extension agent has graciously agreed to judge the competition for White Top and Fairy Rings. Come on up and bring your own weed.

The Architecture of Change

EVERYONE WANTS TO BE in Colorado. We all want to live on the frontier with the sun in our eyes and the wind at our back. And, because there is no border patrol, Newbies will always pour over the mountain passes to taste the sweet life. The hearty ones walked, trailing wagons and children. Today they drive Hummers stuffed with kids who watch DVDs instead of looking out the window.

Truth is, you can fence out cattle but not change, and the West has always been about change: open range vs. fences, cattlemen vs. sheepmen, cows vs. condos, environmentalists vs. everybody. But, as Darwin said, "Suck it up."

History is about moving up against each other's watering holes. Today's push-and-shove is about pretty places and the wealthy, educated, white baby boomers who are inundating them. Pitkin County Commissioner Mick Ireland calls it the Baby Boomer Tsunami and warns everyone to be afraid, very afraid, because it's only the beginning. Demographers tell us there are 73 million baby boomers in America, and some days it feels like every single one of them has moved into my town, although only 1.3 million live in Colorado.

They come because they want to *stay* young. We came into the country in the '60s because we *were* young. We left fancy jobs on both coasts, lived in teepees, and sang along with Waylon and Willie. The bandannas wrapped around our heads matched the kerchiefs on our dogs. Baby boomers want to be entertained, we wanted to be left alone. They want to be safe, we wanted to drink at the VFW. They want land use plans, we wanted to do drugs. They want bike paths, boutiques, and symphonies in the park. We wanted to save the world and have the freedom to say, "I'm gonna shoot my horse, my dog, or my Old Lady," without being reported to social services.

We were the children of the Age of Aquarius. We came to Colorado to make love, avoid war, and fight change. We came because the doctor made house calls and the plumber came when he said he would—and sometimes they were the same guy. We wanted to be mavericks, to fight over fence lines instead of politics. We came so we could cuss, spit chew into empty beer cans, raise pigs in the backyard, buy groceries on credit, drink with the sheriff, and play poker with the mayor. We put two Labs in the back of every pickup, and knew everyone on the police blotter. We ignored the building inspector and fought Wal-Mart.

The new boomers are Lone Eagles, strange, location-neutral birds who can work wherever there is wireless. They are engineers, consultants, and professionals with big brains and big bucks who jet off to big city offices or sell stuff on eBay. A recent study by the Northwest Colorado Council of Governments indicates these wealthy, middle-aged, second-home owners occupy sixty percent of the housing units in the Colorado mountain communities of Eagle, Grand, Pitkin, and Summit Counties. These chaps may write checks to United Way, but they aren't going to join the volunteer fire department. Our kids can't afford to build on the back forty or buy a fixer-upper in town—they either have to leave or become the cleaning ladies, massage therapists, or pest control experts the Newbies depend on. We are raising our young to become hired hands on the land their grandparents homesteaded.

Second-home owners are empty nesters. Why then do their nests have to be so doggone big? Their kids only visit twice a year—to ski at Christmas and tube in summer—so why do they require 7,000-square-foot homes, Olympic-size swimming pools, basketball courts, and movie theatres?

Down at the building department, plan checkers gawk at the architecture of change: bigger windows, synthetic rustic shingles, acres of hardwood and tile, stucco and plaster, trim- and millwork. Inside, security, lighting, shades, climate, and home entertainment centers are remote or automatically controlled. Outside, heated driveways access section-sized portals and patios, engulfed in logs and wrought iron. There is no end to the amount of landscape you can destroy if you are rich.

Where once we fenced out cattle, we now fence to safeguard yard art, artificial waterfalls, irrigation systems, and privately stocked ponds. Forget gated communities, we are gating single-family homes. Fences make it harder to visit with neighbors, so instead of taking fresh-baked banana bread over to welcome a newcomer, we are holding conferences on how to "build community." The only problem is, we may not want the community we are building.

Growing Cash on the Back Forty

I'M LOOKING AT a map of the New West and your spread ain't on it. There's no money in firing up the tractor, and you can't make it selling cows.

Last year Harry cleared $23,000 running cows on an $8 million spread. The views are spectacular but his kid's still going to college on loans, and he's not taking his Old Lady on a Club Med cruise any time soon. Harry says ranchers have to sell out, sell real estate, or come into money. You better be content to live poor and die rich because land values are great for securing loans that are impossible to repay.

Once upon a time you could save the ranch by getting an extension at the bank, working twice as hard, growing your own feed, leasing more land, or having more children. Today, even if you own your spread, you can only expect a two to four percent return on your investment—less than you can get on a CD with no work and no investment.

Up at Dry Lake, the talking heads at chambers, banks, and small business and economic development offices are saying that anyone who thinks what-worked-for-grandpa-will-work-for-me has his shorts over his head. Where we once mined gold, dug coal, and raised live-stock, they're now hawking agri-tourism, heritage-tourism, adventure-tourism, wilderness-tourism, gourmet-tourism, athletic-tourism, and eco-tourism with the zeal of medicine men. "Diversification" and "value added" are the new mantras.

Put a hot tub in the bunkhouse and call it a B&B. Run dudes. Let the kids manage a U-Pick-'Em, and put the Old Lady to work making service berry jellies, soaps, bath salts, and candles. Sell emu oil. Grow stuff that isn't traded on the commodities market. Raise medicinal plants like osha, which sells for ten times the price of hay. Harvest endangered species like Thurber fescue under contract to the Forest Service. Sell spruces, lodgepoles, and chokecherries with landscape value.

Don't cut the crabgrass and then call the back forty a preserve for hunters or photographers. On the web, there's a lady peddling "decorator" tumbleweed, a man shredding aspen bark to use as packing material, and a granny selling toy straw bales that cost more than real ones.

Sell access to Orvis for flyfishing, to American Sportsmen for game hunting, and to the Boy Scouts for field trips. Open a petting zoo, putting green, shooting range. Host tours for birdwatchers and historians. Raise llamas, alpaca, yak, and other exotics. Sell saddles on cattle drives and trail rides. Build a pole barn big enough for nine hundred picnickers to chow down on steaks at reunions and weddings. Dig a nine-foot barbecue pit and throw luaus and nut frys for Kiwanis, Lions, and Rotary.

Fact of the matter is, ranchers and farmers do not play well with others. They are independent SOBs and have every intention of staying that way. They claim they're too dumb to do different. Harry says he's packing it in because the cost of money is too high, and government regulations are stifling. He's tired of working so hard, and his granddaddy would come back to haunt him if he began selling conservation easements, fenced hunting leases, or yee-haw adventures.

Makes you wonder how many pumpkin patches, corn mazes, and hayrides the nation can support. How many times will a person pay to pet a goat? To what extent does the sale of landscapes painted on saw blades impact the gross national product?

More importantly, do you really want your kids to grow up in a roadside stand selling jerky, stick horses, and barbecue sauce? Can you surrender your privacy, hayfields, and front porch to rubber-necking yahoos, whining children and ill-mannered dogs, every one of which needs a restroom? Do you really want to smile eight hours a day and spend the evening around the campfire with a bunch of turkeys?

A continuing U.S. Department of Agriculture National Survey on Recreation and the Environment reports that every year 62 million adults and 20 million school children (nearly one-third of the entire U.S. population) travel an average of eighty miles to find a farm or ranch experience. Travel agents throughout America, who trace these migration routes, say they all lust for Colorado, so, instead of pulling cows, bus in youth groups so they can ride tractors, milk cows, run the horses ragged, and jump up and down on grapes.

If Disney can do it, so can you. You can always use a cattle prod for crowd control. Meanwhile, take a rancher out to lunch, because he may not be around too much longer.

On Rocky Mountain Couth

Colorado Dreaming

TRUTH BE TOLD, northwest Colorado was never wild. I was. I came into the country in a pair of too-tight Wranglers and got the hots for anyone who could ride a bar stool. I wasn't alone. The Corral Club was littered with debutantes from St. Louis, career girls from New York, and psychology majors from San Francisco. Like me, they came west because they loved the smell of pine needles and sweat.

And the Boys at the Bar knew how to sweat. They worked hard and played hard, a trait that scores high on the romantic meter. Most of them built power plants, ski areas, water treatment systems, and fire houses. They could work six tens, but not without bitching. They knew how to make things work—mostly with duct tape, two-by-fours, and plywood stolen from job sites. And they wore hard hats, a major turn on. They could fix a car when it broke an axle, and the disposal when it choked on chicken bones. They built their own horse trailers and ran their own fence. They were handy to have around the house, especially in the bedroom, but not in the kitchen.

This was not the crowd from *GQ*. Most had teeth the color of grass and lost at least one finger in a hay baler. These were not people with well-stocked minds. Many lived independent of thought process; in fact, there was sometimes no indication that they were awake or thinking. No one had ever been late to a meeting because no one had ever gone to one. Some hadn't talked to anyone but a cow in months.

Just last week Jake allowed as how he'd never read a book. "I could," he said, "just never got around to it." But Jake can name every bird, flower, and tree in the Rockies. He can catch a six-pound trout on American cheese, call in an elk from twenty miles, and build his own house. Jake spends a lot of time trying to make sense of things, most of it down at the Corral Club. Like most of the Boys at the Bar, he has every truck the family ever owned stashed along the fence line behind the barn. He saves two of everything ever hauled over the Pass, and he doesn't take himself too seriously.

Jake says life is just one long trail ride. The easiest way to sub-scribe to this philosophy is to jump into the sack with Jake. Jake got lucky pretty regular because the Corral Club is the international head-quarters for the Boots-in-the-Air Club, whose motto is, "If Debbie likes you, she do; if she don't, she won't."

The local gendarme keeps pretty close tabs on Jake and the rest of the Boys at the Bar because they've racked up a few DUIs, but mostly they take the back roads home on Saturday night, and they don't drive over 180 miles an hour on I-70. They grew up in small towns surrounded by sagebrush and antelope. As kids, they shot rabbits, stole chewing gum from Corner Drug, and walked rattle-snakes home using a shoestring for a leash. Outdoors was home. As teenagers, they stole the family car, spent hours dragging main, and did what kids do in the back seat of a Chevy. The A&W was home. As adults they chew, spit, and spend an inordinate amount of time analyzing fishing holes and hunting camps. Their recollections will never be cataloged, their memories never mined. The Corral Club is home.

Like most of us, they want to be bigger than life so they recreate themselves in myth. The Boys at the Bar like myths because facts are boring and everyone wants to be bigger than boring. Every librarian wants to be a little bit Sacagawea. Every drywaller wants to be a little bit Jim Bridger. Of course, the Boys at the Bar want to be John Wayne. They *loved* John Wayne. He was rugged, tough, firm in his beliefs, and loyal to his friends—as were they. He sat as tall in the saddle as they rode on their bar stools. The Duke could track Indians, trounce villains, chase outlaws, and bring law to the frontier. By closing time, the Boys at the Bar felt capable of any of these chores. "One hand tied behind my back," said Jake.

John Wayne was born in a tiny, white frame house on South Second Street in Winterset, Iowa. He was always big: thirteen pounds when he was born and a mega-star when he died seventy-two years later. John always had a way with women. He was delivered by a woman doctor, and married to three women. Of course his parents left farm country for Hollywood when he was three, but that never hurt his swagger. John Wayne invented the Western myth, Pilgrim, and that was good enough for Jake and the Boys at the Bar.

When stomach cancer threw their hero into a coma, Jake went right down to Corner Drug and bought a get well card. The card traveled down the bar so everyone, even the guys in the back booth, could write Howdy or Get Well Soon. The Boys at the Bar threw back a few beers on June 11, 1979, when John Wayne died. First they toasted the Duke for being his own self, and then they toasted Jake for being able to sign his name.

Colorado Roadtrips

EVER SINCE THE FIRST Conestoga wagon headed west from Pennsylvania we've been waxing poetic about road trips. There's something liberating about saddling up for a mini-voyage with no destination, no time frame, and no kids. The Boys at the Bar go on runners pretty regular, mostly in search of booze and broads, while pretending to escape from the law, the Old Lady, or the building inspector.

Threats of winter make fall the best time to scratch the itch, feed the wanderlust, and indulge in windshield time. In Colorado, where snow is called "white gold" and coal "black gold," the real rush for the gold comes in the fall when color transforms mountains and meadows into quilts of yellow, red, and orange. Book clubs go on field trips, soccer teams take off for tournaments, and birders clog the state's scenic and historic byways. If you hike, it's time to visit one of forty-one state parks. If you fish, it's time to check out the state's 168 miles of gold medal streams. Hunters stay home and clean their guns.

There are 82,171 miles of road in Colorado, fifty-nine percent of them unpaved, and autumn is the most glorious time to explore them. The call of the open road blinds us to the price of gas, back-to-school responsibilities, and office deadlines. We lust for places where there are no scones, wine lists, ATM machines, or holistic health centers. We yearn for landscapes where you can't see manmade things and you can shoot stop signs and mailboxes. We want to find pioneer cemeteries, secret places where the telephone line deadheads, and elk calve out. We want to drive into a sunset or out of a rainstorm. We want to get lost.

MBA-types claim "windshield time" wastes energy, depreciates vehicles, and diminishes profit. They say it's expensive, unproductive, and avoidable, but they're wrong. Windshield time is good for the soul. It permits us to exercise the imagination, change filters, vacate mind and body. It provides space to relax and meditate, to remember the past, to find inspiration in new surroundings, to think about the future. It's easy to become so intent upon exercising the body that we fail to make time for the mind to dance in the land of make-believe. Road trips are our "child time" when, like Ferdinand the Bull, we can sit under a tree and smell the flowers.

Real road runners don't know when they have arrived because they don't know where they're going. It is essential to avoid the 25 million websites that supply maps, books, and planning guides for trips. Ignore all the educational, geophysical, and cyber-activated tools for travel. Resist the temptation to take a mountain bike, pack a camera, dress in spandex, or schlep water bottles. Just put a knife and a salt shaker in the glove compartment so you can snack in roadside gardens, turn a John Prine CD up loud, and sing like you are Beverly Sills.

You may want a traveling companion. Thelma had Louise, Steinbeck had Charlie, and Lewis had Clark. But it's fun to travel solo because it gives you time to think about the important things in life. How many towns have streets named for Martin Van Buren? What percent of the gross national product is generated by speeding tickets in forgotten towns? What are people who put plastic deer in their front yards trying to say? Why does a root beer always taste better at Dairy Queen? Will the motel provide a fly swatter instead of a telephone? Is there any relationship between an open range and a closed mind?

Travel slowly. Explore country where a community is judged by the size of its grain elevator, and guys not only know what sorghum is, they keep close tabs on its market price. Search for a place beyond the reach of public radio, with no library, where everyone can recite the 4-H pledge. Read every historic marker, eat at the greasy spoon, and visit with someone driving a tractor. Find the town where high school football jocks lobbed a drunk chicken across the end zone at half-time.

As my pal Noreen is so fond of pointing out, a good run is better than a bad stand. Runners create space to breathe deep, air out the mind, and explore wide-open meadows, white-topped peaks, and black forests. Politicians promote road maps, coaches encourage life maps, and birders compile life lists. The rest of us, who know there is no road map for life, find a little windshield time can remind us to hang on to the steering wheel.

Colorado Chic

IN COLORADO, we wear clothes that double as camouflage and bedding. We layer them and we sweat in them. We ski in our bathing suits and swim in the altogether. We fish in vests and wear orange to drink. Our boots are steel-toed and our underwear is silk. We dress for extreme heat on the plains and extreme cold in the mountains. Everything we own is waterproof, sun proof, and freeze proof. Mostly we wear jeans.

According to the Statistical Abstract, every man, woman, and child in greater America spends $600 on clothes per year. Not so in Colorado, where we invest far more in dogs and bikes than we do in fashion. Our dogs, and we prefer yellow Labs, eat better than we do, and we lay out more for our bikes than we do for our mortgages. In

Colorado, chic is chaps, not Sherpa. We sleep in flannel nighties, not Victoria's Secret. We wear bright red long johns and truly evil sports bras with four-inch-wide straps.

We live in a world of Gortex, spandex, and fleece. We talk about where we buy our socks at the dinner table. Sometimes we act like ours is the only state in the union that has pine trees, mountains, and trout, not to mention water. Our clothes reflect who we are, not who we want to be. And let's face it, we do spend a lot of time shoveling roofs, attending pie socials, and draining beaver ponds. We're thrilled when we receive glove and boot dryers for Christmas. We've traded fashion for fitness.

Our closets, basements, attics, and garages are stuffed with helmets for kayaking, biking, and rock climbing. And with gloves for shooting, cycling, and racquetball. They are full of bikes with 117 gears, 5 BR/3 BA campers, 80-man rafts, and 17-burner grills. Our shelves are packed with paddles and pitons, lures and hitches, binoculars and branding irons. Everything we own is biodegradable and held together with duct tape. We don't patronize stores that carry toe-less, sling-back, spike-heeled pumps.

We are what we wear, and in Colorado we are gearheads—we are obsessed with the outdoors. The amount of time we spend outdoors is a status symbol, doesn't matter whether you're riding a backhoe or a baler, skiing or walking the dog, as long as you're weathering the elements, turning your skin to leather. Somehow we feel compelled to challenge heights, depths, and Mother Nature. We mortgage our homes to buy equipment that promises survival. We devote every moment we're not gawking at the Broncos to perusing catalogs for sporting goods and guides, quads and weapons, bug repellants and pedometers. Devices used to measure temperature, barometric pressure, and altitude are especially prized. Moisturizer is essential.

When a child is born back East, his parents wait-list him for Harvard. In the Rockies, we sign him up for a trip down the Grand Canyon. Waiting lists suggest it might be his graduation present, but, in the meantime, he can be collecting gear: boots for riding, branding, and dancing; waders for walking ditch lines, cleaning septic tanks, and fishing; sneakers for tennis, jogging, and yachting; skis for downhill, cross country, and jumping.

In the real West, only dogs wear bandannas. A guy can get along nicely with one tie, probably left over from his wedding, and most gals long ago cut the feet out of their last pair of pantyhose to keep the dog from getting knocked up. Natives ski in overalls, have raccoon eyes from ski goggles, and protect their noses with zinc oxide. Too macho to wear sun block in summer, their complexions rust. Real cowboys sport oversized hats held up by splayed ears, vests decorated with elk teeth, and $3 clip-on sunglasses from the truck stop. And their socks are dirty, you can bet on it.

Wannabe Westerners tuck designer jeans into knee-high Noconas, wear $300 Bolles and shearling coats from Overland Sheepskin. This is the perfect outfit for going into town to buy a $400 chain saw and an $80,000 Range Rover to cut a cord of wood that costs $120 cut, delivered, and stacked.

Down at the Corral Club, the boys are still shaking their heads about Mary Jane from Chicago, who finagled her way into hunting camp wearing a fur coat. Damn lucky she didn't get shot, they say.

Come to think on it, love of gear may be the only thing old timers and newcomers have in common. They all have a penchant for accumulating stuff, just not the same stuff.

Colorado Romance

NOBODY SAYS "I love you" more convincingly than a prairie chicken. Mockingbirds sing, peacocks strut, bowerbirds build elaborate nests, egrets grow feathers, but prairie chickens do it best. They dance and croon at dawn and dusk. They lean forward, puff up their throat and ear feathers, drop their wings, and fan their tails.

The sound of air rushing from their inflated, bright-orange neck sacs makes a booming sound as they stomp their feet and strut around in circles, not unlike a Bronco quarterback after a touchdown.

The best place to watch the mating dance of greater prairie chickens is in the grassy sandhills, north of Wray, where eighty percent of Colorado's ten thousand chickens hang out, near the Kansas and Nebraska state lines. The numbers come close to matching the people population in Yuma County, which issued only seventy-three marriage licenses last year, suggesting that prairie chickens may have far more fun courting in the cornfields than do the locals.

Their eerie sounds and aerial leaps are generating economic development for the Wray Chamber of Commerce and East Yuma County Historical Society that, from mid-March until mid-May, haul voyeurs to the booming grounds. There, squinting into the cold and the dark, bird watchers and snoops can spy on roosters and hens cavorting on the lek under the educated eyes of Division of Wildlife yentas. The ruckus attracts females from five miles away and tourists from around the globe.

Like good men, prairie chickens are hard to find. They hide in the brush, claim a territory, and protect it from other males. They fight frequently but most face-offs are bluffs. The most dominant bird claims the center of the booming grounds, a hilltop meadow with a good view of any approaching predators. When a hen enters the lek, the males run toward her and, ignoring territorial boundaries, position themselves to stomp, boom, cackle, jump, and bow. It looks a lot like the Corral Club at closing time.

Mating is chauvinistic and promiscuous. After booming, the Casanovas return to the lek and continue to display. In winter they flock up because there's safety in numbers, but while females migrate long distances, males remain near the booming grounds, not unlike the Boys at the Bar who, unless some hen pries them off, can perch on the same bar stool for twenty years.

Scholars have always been interested in how men troll for women. They devoted a decade to discovering that giardia have a sex life, but only recently did a pair of anthropologists move their research on the mating behavior of apes into bars, not a quantum leap. In a recent article in a learned journal on evolution and behavior, these researchers concluded that guys attract gals with macho male body language, by stroking their beards, punching their male friends, or sprawling across furniture with legs akimbo. The key to scoring, they explained, lies in males shooting repeated glances at females, an average of thirteen times in a half hour for those who landed dates. Because the study was not federally funded, it failed to examine the impact of jewelry, furs, yachts, and cars on courting.

The best place to witness human mating rituals is when the last call sounds down at the local watering hole. That's when the Boys at the Bar begin to preen, strut, and squawk. They convince themselves that, with just one more round, they can slay dragons, swim moats, and survive duels. They attempt to persuade any damsel within earshot that only she can feel the pea under the mattress, spin flax into gold, and remain beautiful forever.

After enough brewskis they are ready to round up twelve goats, the tail of a white sheep, or some dried dove's tongues. Truth be told, Harry is worn out from running around the countryside looking for a lost slipper, and Agnes is tired of kissing frogs, so they agree to exchange e-mails.

Nowadays, love is found in cyberspace, defined in a pre-nuptial agreement, and consummated with a glacier-sized rock. The rules of catch-and-release have changed. The search for keepers now takes place in gourmet groceries and continuing ed classes, at museums and libraries, on trips up ski lifts and the Himalayas. Hanging out at hardware stores and airport baggage claim roundabouts are proving some of the best modern booming grounds.

Today, the fanciest courting may occur not in Colorado's fifteen thousand bars, but on the state's seven hundred leks, where prairie chickens, once endangered, are demonstrating how to perpetuate the species without benefit of cards and candy.

Colorado Winters

COLORADO WINTERS can be tough. They clutter garages with so many skis, boards, sleds, inner tubes, and toboggans that there is no room for a car. Snow closes roads and schools. It causes avalanches, glaciers, and floods. It snarls traffic and makes snowplow drivers crabby, so they plow your driveway closed—unless, of course, you are a county commissioner.

Ralph Waldo Emerson, Herodotus, and Robert Service wrote about winter without dwelling on chapped lips, hypothermia, and frostbite. When Good King Wenceslas "looked out"—he didn't see ice dams in roof gutters, tree branches on top of cars, and eighteen-wheelers flipped on the interstate. He was not forced to fight frozen locks and gas caps or scrape windshields with a credit card. He saw soft, pure, silent, dancing white flakes—and he thought about clouds of geese, not frozen nose hairs.

Champagne powder slows life and allows you time to think about important stuff: where to go on spring vacation, when to go on the Atkins diet, or whether or not to divorce the Old Man. Snow makes you want to read poetry in front of a roaring fire, make brownies, and drink black Russians. It invokes memories of ice falls along Clear Creek, snow-dusted evergreens on the Lariat Loop Trail, and chimichangas at the Wondervu Café in Coal Creek Canyon. Snow provides the mental health days essential to surviving yet another Mud Season.

Kids love snow because they can stay toasty and watch TV indoors, or they can go outside and turn blue building snowmen and making snow angels. Hunters like the snow because it helps them track game. Dads have time to listen to weather reports and ponder the pros and cons of salt, scoria, chains, studs, and snow tires. Moms get "couch time" to peruse seed catalogs for snow peas, snow-drops, and snow-on-the-mountain. And by day three everyone has Cabin Fever.

Ski bums and bunnies like snow because they can lounge around moss-rock fireplaces telling lies and making out. Dentists thrive because flying hockey pucks knock out so many teeth, and since they started building furniture out of snow fence, interior decorators flourish. The Type-A Gortex Crowd is busy skiing, boarding, sledding, skijoring, and cutter racing. Linguists debate how many words the Eskimos have for snow, while entrepreneurs at the nation's 490 ski areas throw elaborate Sno Balls. Geeks browse 19.2 million sites devoted to snow, including one selling a musical snow globe that tosses miniature skiers about when you "click and drag."

Up at Dry Lake, teenage girls spend Saturday evenings waiting for their boyfriends to pull tourists out of snow banks to acquire enough tip money to finance a date. Winter is a happy time for everyone except mailmen, auto mechanics, road crews, slope-maintenance people, and ambulance and search and rescue types. The state patrol and tow truck operators cope, unlike snowbirds who just hie off to Arizona. Somewhere around the age of seventy-three, they tend to tire of sitzmarks and faceplants, and start using a ski pole to hobble about town.

Currier and Ives got it all wrong. Their pictures of a rugged woodsman, packing his trusty rifle and four dead ducks into the rosy glow of a snow-covered cabin, give no indication that he planned to clean them in the sink. There is no hint that his cherub-faced children made sleds from every turkey pan, cookie sheet, trash bag, and scrap of wax paper in the house. There is no clue that his Old Lady is going to kill him because his faithful dog tracked mud all over the kitchen floor.

Up in the High Country, where exhaustive research indicates snow can make you depressed, thirsty, or both, the most effective energizers are hot toddies, hot chocolate, wassail, or beverages loaded with cinnamon sticks. Irish whiskey is an especially good pick-me-up because it contains the four basic food groups: sugar, caffeine, alcohol, and whipped cream. Warm drinks equip you to tackle the traffic on I-70, hostile natives, and legendary snow snakes.

Colorado is where the Tenth Mountain Division trained and we're still doing battle: Dads with snow blowers, ranchers with baling wire, cross-country skiers with snowmobilers, and snowplow operators with street round-abouts. Skijockeys continue to challenge nailjockeys for elbow room at the bar.

Snow demands patience. We are either hauling it off or piling it up to celebrate winter carnivals or snow-sculpture competitions. We waste a lot of time standing around until a kid finds his mittens, someone tracks down the Carmex, or Ed Green gets the forecast right. We are forever waiting for snowplows to clear Vail Pass, for the end of a white-out on Rabbit Ears, for sand trucks to hit Wolf Creek Pass, or for I-70 to open at Limon.

Down at the Corral Club, the Boys at the Bar are still reliving the big freezes. The jury's still out on which was the Big One: the 1886 blizzard that froze most of the cattle in the northwest; 1940, when Denver's George Cranmer got the idea to turn snow into "white gold" by opening Winter Park; or 2003, when 258 roofs failed to survive snow loads. Regardless of the year, you can bet it will be "last March."

They remember when the ducks on City Park Pond were anchored in ice; when Leadville boasted an Ice Palace; the time it dumped on Grand Lake in June and on Frisco's July Fourth Parade. They are still talking about the homeless guy who wintered in a mini-storage unit, and the youngster who was impaled on a dagger icicle. Snow is good, they say, because we love sending all that water to green-up lawns in Phoenix and Vegas, and without it, all those liberals in Los Angeles might wither away.

Colorado Pack Rats

OUT WHERE THE D&RGW hangs a left, where everyone is on septic and cooks in cast iron, we judge time in minutes instead of miles. We sit around listening to old farts telling stories, and we spend bunches of time discussing the weather. We also accumulate things that are of no practical use.

It's not that we collect things, we just don't throw them away. Not even after they yellow with age, rust from exposure, or disappear in dust. Our lofts, sheds, and barns are stuffed with our most favorite things: miniatures and milk glass, cookie cutters and comics, parasols and petite point, quilts and piano shawls, all insulation for attics and Section 8 housing for moths.

We are enthralled by age as long as it applies to things and not people. Doesn't matter whether we have any use for it, or even like it. Old stuff is good, meaningful, beautiful, and valuable. Assuming old things were made in mysterious ateliers by talented artisans sipping port, we relish vintage gewgaws.

We are convinced our shards will be worth a fortune on eBay, or when the *Antiques Road Show* pulls into town. We are consumed with guilt at parting with anything a great-grandmother made from the baptism gowns of forty-seven dead cousins. We hang on to stuff because it will be the pièce de résistance at a garage sale, or we convince ourselves that our kids will someday need it. Of course, Junior left home twenty years ago and never returned to clean a closet, much less haul off his Lionel trains.

My pal Gwen collected frogs on the theory that, if she could kiss enough of them, one would turn into a prince. She had frogs on every vase, paperweight, pin cushion, and pendant. There were lily pads in the foyer and stuffed animals in the bedroom. By the time a Sugar Daddy came a courtin', her place looked like a frogatorium at the Botanical Garden.

Out at Dry Lake I've been "making" antiques for years. I've got vintage-in-the-works all over the property: old *National Geographics* in the living room, a mangle in the basement, a '47 Plymouth behind the garage, trunks full of Barbies and Barneys in the tool shed, an 1886 Winchester in the closet, and Beatles memorabilia in the guest room. My rec room is littered with marbles and stamps, Styrofoam cups and Happy Meal wrappers, shirts with fringe, and plastic plants. I claim this is because I want to be prepared for any antique-thirsty collector of dusty treasures who may stop by, not because I am a lousy housekeeper.

My antique of choice is cream of tartar cans. I buy the stuff to make some impress-the-company kind of dessert and promptly forget why it's taking up shelf space. Every five years I stash the can in the garage and paint over the oblong scar on the kitchen shelf. Within weeks, sometimes days, a new recipe will require a dash or a pinch, but certainly no more than 1/4 teaspoon of the stuff. So back I go to Aisle 4 to purchase another tin, wondering why the missing ingredient is always cream of tartar. Why not tamarind, coriander, or cardamom?

Cream of tartar poses a lot of nagging questions—not as many as world peace, but enough to challenge. Why do I never have it when I need it, never need it when I have it? How essential can ingredients measured in elfin quantities really be? What would happen if I left it out? Did Julia Child have this problem? What is it anyway?

Come to find out, cream of tartar is potassium bitartrate, a natural baking powder made from fermented sediment in the bottom of wine barrels. If you don't intend to devote an entire can to stiffening egg whites for Key lime pie, rhubarb soufflé, or snicker-doodles, the rest of the container can be used to make Play-doh, tenderize meat, or bleach your collection of Victorian hankies and Edwardian lingerie.

We assume collectors know something worth knowing. We think the powers-that-be might close the Pass and we'll never again find a hand-fired angel, fairy, or cherub. When you live ninety miles from groceries, you hang on to stuff for good reasons. You're too far from town to run for parts. You want to preserve a little something for posterity. And you still believe that she who dies with the most feather dusters, wins.

Colorado Matchmaking

I'm thinkin' about hooking up with Fred-the-Electrician because I'm tired of watching cowboys ride into the sunset without me. I'm sick of stories about divorced brides, older brides, brides with children who might not like his children, brides with cats who don't get along with his dogs. I'm lookin' to write vows, make a bouquet from ribbons stuck in a paper plate, and slam cake into a smiling face. And no matter what anyone says, I'm going to save the wedding dress, even though I'll never fit into it again.

Fred loves weddings. Makes no difference whether he has ever laid eyes on the parties involved. He marches into churches just to watch the ceremonies. He once danced the night away at a remote bar, pinning so many ten dollar bills on the bride, a total stranger, that the groom called in the local gendarmes. When a pal failed to invite him to usher at his wedding, Fred ordered a tux from the local clothing store, charged it to the bride's father, and stood up for the groom, uninvited. At another wedding gala he stole an entire place setting from the dinner, returning it to the young marrieds, piece by piece, as anniversary gifts for the next ten years. Fred's my kinda guy.

My pal Margaret Jane says she wants no part of seating charts and guest lists, flowers and invitations, catering and limousines, music and rings. She likes the idea that Eskimos face matrimony armed with one pot. So she's planning to register her name at the courthouse and her gift choices at the co-op. What she really wants is a side of beef, cut and wrapped to her specifications, and a Barcalounger in which to watch virtual weddings on TV.

So I'm ready to take the first step toward living happily ever after: overcoming the stress, tension, and uncertainty of a wedding ceremony. This will surely require vast quantities of tranquilizers, alcohol, and chocolate—but I'm sure the groom's heebie-jeebies and my zits will clear before our tenth anniversary. Under the tutelage of counselors, consultants, and investment brokers armed with websites, Palm Pilots, and pre-nup agreements, I can wrestle the tough decisions.

I will skirt the bridal land mines: whether to exchange vows in a vineyard, under a waterfall, during a hayride, on Rollerblades, sky diving, scuba diving, while going up in a hot air balloon, or coming down a ski slope. I don't want to think about how to prevent the blood samples from freezing on the way to Denver; what goes on top of the cake; what to do with the goldfish swimming around in the flower vases on each table; how to dispose of the moose head from his brother in Alaska.

The average engagement lasts sixteen months and I will devote every one of them to analyzing what to do if the priest forgets to show up, the minister is late, or the rabbi gets lost. I can handle the mother-in-law who threatens suicide a week before the ceremony, or the caterer who should; whether to show cleavage; how to conceal eyes puffy from crying; the ramifications of throwing rice, wheat, or birdseed without an environmental impact statement.

I'm determined to survive the mind-cramping decisions occasioned by finding a ring in the Kleenex box. It just requires a few basic decisions: To spend the next fifty years attempting to reconcile the fact that diamonds are a girl's best friend with the reality that a man's best friend is his dog. To buy a house, build a family, bury each other's parents, and to love, honor, and respect each other till death or divorce do you part. To name your first born after his ne'er-do-well grandfather; to transform your mother into a mother-in-law; allow your father access to the bathroom; and turn a frog into a prince.

Every year more than 2.5 million couples tie the knot in churches, city halls, chapels, and backyards throughout America. They invest more than $40 billion in flowers and favors, tiaras and gowns, toasting glasses and silver-plated cake servers. They drop another $4 billion on honeymoons in Vegas, Disneyland, and Maui. They spend one percent of the gross national product so Uncle Charlie can get sloshed; Aunt Erma can have heat stroke waiting for the photographer to finish posing pictures; and the family can visit with your future father-in-law's first three wives, every one of them dressed in beige. But let's face it, no amount of money can assure that someone will dance with your cousin Marlene.

On Cowboys

Eulogy for a Cowboy

MEN WEPT OPENLY at his wake because, as Crazydave-the-Plumber insisted, he had it all: a good horse, a good dog, and a good woman. Nothing was to be gained by questioning the order. His pal Mike hosted the memorial service in front of a huge bonfire at his Three Quarter Circles Ranch west of town. Jay-the-Fireman poured champagne into Crazydave's cowboy hat and passed it around the circle so everyone could cry in it or make a final toast.

It was a nippy October afternoon and my best bud Chris Ensworth, who left a convent to run the Hiway Bar before buying a small-town newspaper, gave the eulogy. Her words reflected the laughter, friendship, and love common to men in the West. She began by quoting Sam Foss.

Bring me men to match my mountains,
Bring me men to match my plains,
Men with empires in their purpose,
And new eras in their brains.

Crazydave-the-Plumber was one of those men, she said. His spirit matched the mountains and the plains, the seasons and the wind that has hewn the land.

The spirit of the mountains is not a birthright, nor is it deeded with the land, rather it is earned with grit and steadfastness. At times it is a test of physical strength or intelligence, but always it is a test of individual will against the challenge at hand. Do not mourn for Dave, he reveled in the gifts of life.

He knew work. Forty degrees below zero or a hundred degrees above, he knew the satisfaction of hard physical labor, the smell of his own sweat, and how to get the job done and done right.

He knew pain. It could be delivered from a horse that had pulled him in the dirt or by a foe who had whacked him on the nose.

He knew happiness. A blazing fire, talking and laughing with friends and family, washing it all down with the taste of a cold Coors.

He knew sorrow. It came with the death of friends and family and it laid on the cold earth with shattered hopes and dreams.

He knew joy. The smell of fall, the feel of winter wind, the pleasure of a good horse underneath, and a rifle in hand.

He knew what to cherish. That included hunting season, fixing old ladies' sinks, taking kids to rodeos, and cheating on the building inspector.

He was as good as his word. Getting a job done may have been a priority, but taking time to help a neighbor was always more important. What other people thought, petty posturing by lesser men, and errant toilets in the driveway were of no concern.

He knew love. From his friends and family, the Old Lady, and the kids who hung out in his backyard.

Crazydave knew life. He nurtured it and reaped from it. He had a strong spirit and a true heart. He had his code: right was right, and wrong was to be set right. And in his own way and in his own time, he tried to right what wrongs he could. Crazydave was, in the truest sense of the word, a straight shooter.

He knew that in this game called life you climb on the horse, plant your feet firmly in the stirrups, and take your very best grip. You grit your teeth and, with spurs ready, leave the gate. You do not know, with each twist, turn, and blow that fate delivers, whether you will hear the buzzer or just end in a heap, picking dirt from your teeth. But when it is all over and the dust settles, you have one more adventure under your belt and a helluva story to tell.

Native American warriors believe that every day is a good day to die. The flip side of that philosophy is that every day is a good day to live. Crazydave knew his days. So, do not mourn for Dave; he lived a full, generous, and abundantly ornery life, brimming with laughter and love. He is one of the men who matched the mountains.

After a few good stories and a bucket of tears, everyone blew hard into their kerchiefs and adjourned to the VFW, where we emptied a few kegs trying to figure out who in hell *is* Sam Foss?

Their Lifestyle

COWBOYS AREN'T MY weakness. I married the guy Sarah Lawrence chicks lust after, and the truth of the matter is, cowboys look best in roping arenas and poorly lit bars. Mostly they have bad teeth, foot rot, and emphysema. They spit chew into empty beer cans and leave skid marks in their shorts. They don't take their boots off when they come into the house. They don't take their hats off when they eat dinner, and they don't take their long johns off when they climb into bed.

They begin the day with an unfiltered cigarette and coffee laced with whiskey, and they end it with red beer. They never mop the stove after fixin' bacon and eggs. Some have never read a hardback book, and most are politically to the right of Aaron Burr. They don't talk much, but they look you straight in the eye when they do, which is irresistible. It is equally admirable that they can get out of bed in the morning no matter what transpired the night before. There's something fascinating about a guy who can spend twelve hours perched on a bar stool debating Ford vs. Chevy, Bud vs. Coors, Anyone vs. the Raiders.

Cowboys are supposed to be heroes, knights, cavemen, swashbuckling men of honor and few words, bigger than life. It's the Code of the West. He's going to ride in and save the day, but try getting him to take out the trash. He's sensitive to the needs of animals, but it never occurs to him that you need your back rubbed. He knows how to tend to the land, but he can't remember your birthday. He can shoot an elk at two hundred yards, but he can't hit the toilet at two feet.

This may be because cowboys are raised without benefit of psychoanalysis, Prozac, or other civilizing influences such as mothers. Mom was, one hears tell, wondrous wise, an extraordinary cook, and a candidate for sainthood for putting up with Dad. So how's come he left home at fourteen? And why didn't she teach Bucko to separate the whites from the darks?

Cowboy testosterone assures that a guy will open bean cans with a knife, deposit cigarette ashes in the cuff of his jeans, and blow his nose on the ground. He will fart in public and in bed. He feels "shit" says 'bout everything that needs to be said, and he never loses interest in jokes about sheep.

You hear they've found a new use for sheep? Naw. Yep, growing wool.
  Well, shit.
We're outta' Bud. Oh, shit.
Cows got through the fence. Aw, shit.
Erna left for good this time. No shit?
Martians just landed on the back forty. Bullshit!

I'm not shittin' ya' girls, cowboys have no intention of establishing a relationship with anyone other than their dog. They would just as soon snuggle up with a .30-30. They covet no worldly possessions other than an American-made pickup. They live in mobile homes with trampled green shag carpet, a sink full of dirty dishes, and a broken recliner. The bathroom hasn't been scrubbed in a decade. The pickup, on the other hand, gets Golden Door treatment.

My very own personal cowboy hailed from Nowhere, Wyoming. Like most everybody from Wyoming, he bellowed, "Powder River, let 'er buck!" upon entering a bar. He roped the furniture, and strapped rigging on the coffee table to teach the neighborhood kids how to buck. He never called when he was going to be late for dinner—and, in fact, sometimes forgot to come home at all. He moved the poker game into the dining room the minute I left to visit my mother.

He put ketchup on everything except watermelon and considered a toothpick an integral part of every meal. Because he hated the neighbors, he only trimmed the tree branches shading our side of the property line. He decorated a buddy's wedding reception with a gross of condoms filled with helium.

I'm here to tell ya'—sitting on the tailgate while your Old Man rides Jackpot Rodeo gets lonely. Hearing his ribs crack when he falls off a bull gets old. Waiting for the Corral Club to serve the last round so you can chauffeur him to the emergency room can become a bore. So, get real girls. Miss Kitty never washed socks. Cowboys love their roping partners more than they're ever gonna love you. And if you ever hook up with one, keep the life insurance paid up because you're probably gonna kill him.

Their Virtues and Vices

COWBOYS HAVE AN affinity for sorry-ass teenage boys. They get along quite well because both are convinced that being in trouble is a function of being alive. Cowboys can handle fistfights in the parking lot, midnight keggers, and DUIs. Politicians and long hairs slow 'em down a bit, but drugs, unemployment, and getting caught are totally out of the question.

The Boys at the Bar want to believe life is simple and we were put here to have a good time. They see no pressing need to fritter away time searching for profound truths when time is better spent hunting and fishing. No point in standing around waiting for the road to widen. Nothing to be gained by watching cement harden. This philosophy frees vast amounts of time to watch the Denver Broncos, which is enormously appealing to teenage boys.

Teenage Stomps wear muddy boots, repair fence, and poach deer. Teenage Freaks wear alligator boots, kayak, and have daddies willing to pay their bail. Cowboys say you can drink with either crowd, but they want the youth of America to grow up to be backhoe operators and automobile mechanics. Local cops are less optimistic about what their future holds. Up at Dry Lake, the police department buys two copies of the high school yearbook to have the kids' mug shots handy, just in case.

The Boys at the Bar want their kids to be somebody, do something, even if it's wrong. They encourage capers with class. Class has nothing to do with money, education, or lineage. It's about imagination, style, and stories. No one knew who toilet-papered the teacher's lounge, but everyone agreed it was not classy. Doug was nailed for lobbing rocks out of a treehouse at a police car. No class. Larry forgot to bring along matches when he attempted to set fire to a city sign. No class. But he wouldn't rat on his buddies. That's class.

After drinking beer in the backyard until two in the morning, Billy got arrested for impersonating a hood ornament. That's class. Henry shot out the revolving bucket on the roof of KFC because it blocked the view of the mountains from Main Street. That's class. No one knew who blew up the CBI van housing the narcs, but everyone agreed it was a class act.

Crazydave-the-Plumber was a classy kinda guy. He got thrown in the slammer for drunk walking. He had two watches, one for daylight savings and one for standard time. When the optometrist, who doubled as a local bartender, told him he needed glasses, he made the doctor buy him shots. Crazydave liked my mother because she was the Queen of Class. In her company he morphed into Little Lord Fauntleroy. He cleaned up his language, walked her poodle, and acquired a smattering of French.

He would insist that we dine al fresco, although more frequently than not, it meant in the garage. He refined the art of flambé. On Thanksgiving he set the turkey on fire, on Christmas he set the cherries on fire, and on New Year's he set the chair on fire, but that was because he fell asleep holding a lit cigarette. He also became enamored of tossing champagne glasses into the fireplace after elaborate toasts, wiping out the Waterford a generation too soon. On more than one occasion, he missed the fireplace entirely, but as the French would no doubt agree, it's the thought that counts.

Although scores of relatives from back East shipped their preppy kids west for summer-long plumbing apprenticeships, none entered the profession. The paperboy, forced to sing seasonally appropriate songs when he came to collect, is now an EMT. One became a priest, another a dentist. Through the years Crazydave took every one of them down to a Friday Night Jackpot Rodeo and sat them down on bulls, unbeknownst to their mothers. Riding a bull was a rite of passage.

It's how you become a man, he told our daughter's pasty-face sophomoric boyfriend. Chuck's ride was short. The gate opened, the boyfriend hit the ground, Crazydave helped him to his feet, and off they went to the Corral Club for a couple or three beers. Chuck-the-Boyfriend grew up to be an aeronautical engineer, and no questions asked, it was because he fell off a bull.

Crazydave said Jimmy-the-Stonemason was a bona fide class act. Jimmy spent Septembers walking the Dry Lake drainage in search of a black bear. No bait, no dogs, just glasses and patience. For five years he scouted oak brush, chokecherries, and berries searching for sign. For five years the bear contained his natural curiosity about his hunter and the brightly colored ribbons he tied to tree branches. Jimmy and the bear got to know each other pretty well—what they ate, when they slept, and where they pooped in the woods.

Jimmy says that bagging that bear, after all those years, made him sad, same as a divorce or a death in the family. Of course, he sought solace down at the Corral Club, where he cried in his beer because, as the Boys at the Bar will tell you, life's about the adventure, not the trophy.

Their Design

THE WESTERN DESIGN CONFERENCE isn't about the way we live out at Dry Lake. There are no oil-cloth tablecloths, no gun racks, and no sand-filled coffee cans for Marlboro butts. There are no crocheted cozies, plastic sofa covers, TV trays, or cuckoo clocks. No dartboards, mounted jackalope heads, or flashing neon signs assuring that the bar is open. There are no dingoes sitting in the back of pickups patiently waiting for their owners, and no one rides a horse into a bar. It is solid boutiques and Brie.

In Cody, Wyoming, where the Western Design Conference is held every September, wild means wildly expensive. It certainly doesn't mean Jell-O salad, pickled eggs, and jerky. The women all look like Madonna, and most of the men tuck their jeans into knee-high cowboy boots made from the skin of alligators, snakes, and zebras. Everyone drinks Bordeaux instead of Bud. No one spits chew into topless beer cans, blows their nose directly into the grass, or talks dirty. There is fringe everywhere: on jackets, hats, furniture, and curtains.

They gather right down on Stampede Avenue to showcase the "best" western fashions, furnishings, and architecture in juried exhibitions, educational seminars, and runway fashion shows with models coiffed by the likes of Paul Mitchell. This is quilts and antler art gone haute couture. It is impossible to tell the craftsmen, decorators, architects, and high-end retailers from the customers, owners of million-dollar, multi-acre third homes. This crowd doesn't hang at wet T-shirt contests or get 86'd from bars. They read the *New York Times*, not Zane Gray. They wear Cassini, not Carharts, and they make small talk over delicate morsels of marinated mountain lion and rattlesnake.

The Western Design Conference is for people who live in houses with white carpet. Exhibit halls are filled with stuff the co-op doesn't carry: chairs made from tree branches, dressers built from snow fence, tables crafted from Olympic-size slabs of polished pine, pool tables and bar stools carved from enough trees to furnish a national forest. Why is it decorators feel we need bears and coyotes strolling through pine trees on our headboards? Moose holding up lampshades? Sheepwagons furnished with flowered quilts and bolsters? Personally I've never wanted to curl up in a wing chair upholstered in Hereford; I know too many cowboys who would delight in sliding a cowpie under the seat.

Exhibitors at the Western Design Conference don't put old tires on the roof to keep it from blowing away. They don't line the driveway with plumbing parts. They don't station a vintage John Deere at the front door. Instead, they employ the ancient Chinese art of feng shui to create an environment that is supposed to promote love, increase prosperity, and eliminate failure. One year a feng shui interior designer, flown in from California, encouraged everyone to rearrange their furniture and possessions so the energy patterns are in harmony with chi or life force.

I was afraid to ask her how to cope with the chicken living under the front porch, seven dog bowls on the back porch, and two toilets and a sink in the driveway. Or the Christmas tree, dead since March, blocking the garden gate, the fourteen tons of hay hampering access to the garage, the rusted oil drums in the corral, faded towels in the bathroom, Lava soap in the kitchen, and Grandma's doilies on the sofa arms.

Forget the yin and yang, my Old Man is never going to put the potty lid down, toss the blue tin coffee cups, or sit in anything other than his ratty maroon lounger. There's no way I could install a gurgling fountain or a window box full of greening bamboo shoots. There's no way the marriage would last if I asked him to park his pickup out of sight, move his welding outfit, or soap the tack in the shed instead of in the living room. He likes the kids' drawings cluttering the refrigerator door.

I'm thinking how to explain the life-enhancing advantages of feng shui to the guys at the Corral Club. They might have trouble with the chimes, crystals, mirrors, and goldfish, always red and in multiples of nine. They might balk at adjustments suggested by the feng shui lady: red sheets on the bed to inject passion into life, red carpet in the front hall to encourage friendship, and a red front door to encourage wealth. Sounds an awful lot like a bordello, I'm thinking, so I'll just stick with red beer.

Their Poetry

LET'S FACE IT, not all Westerners ride rodeo and write poetry, but the ones who do spend January sharing laughter and lies at the National Western Stock Show in Denver and the National Cowboy Poetry Gathering in Elko, Nevada. When snow covers the third fence wire, rural folk and cattle people, packers and stockyard execs, auctioneers and artisans, cowboys and wannabes find time to buck and shoot the breeze.

January is when the boys in the big hats rendezvous to eat big steaks and tell big lies. It's the season to mend harness and celebrate the Best of the West. The West's premier rodeo, horseshow, and live-stock event has been celebrated in Denver's Stockyards since 1906, when the Grand Champion steer sold for 33 cents a pound, 23 cents over market price. January is also the season for poets, storytellers, and musicians to gather in Elko to bend an elbow, toast the fallen, count wrinkles, and recite "The Man from Snowy River."

At the Denver Stockyards, they analyze the sex life of sheep, the age of tractors, the agility of stock dogs, and halter styles for yak. They watch professional bull riding and jaw about wind-powered ranch equipment, while ogling the Westernaires and judging feeder calves, horses, and Boer goats. More'n 600,000 broads and buckaroos will be reining and mutton bustin', doggin' and drinkin', buying and selling breeder stock.

In Elko, poets and songsters lasso words, fertilize sentences, and cultivate metaphors. People who would rather listen to rhyming verse than read the Dow Jones will down a few at the Stray Dog on Fifth Street, dine at the Hide-A-Way Steakhouse on Broad, and perform at a convention center not too far from a huge billboard pic-turing Tex telling Bob he has emphysema as they ride into the sunset. Mostly they sing "Strawberry Roan."

Everyone will wear something they shot and talk cowboy. In the New West, you can be a cowboy by sticking your jeans in your boots, sporting fringe, and keeping your hat on at the dinner table. You just have to drive a pickup, shop at the co-op, and hook your thumbs in your front pockets.

Rodeo riders all hail from towns that didn't make the map. They have shot a bear, cheated on the wife, and stopped a stampede. Cowboy poets have always lost everything: their true love, horse, ranch, trail, and herd. Most have moved, without a lot of practice, from crooning to cows to performing for audiences, and all dedicate their rhymes to their mothers, sweethearts, and horses.

You know the plot. He's gonna fall off his horse, ride into the sunset, get soused at Rose's Cantina, and bury his true love. He'll mourn the death of a faithful old dog, tame a wild mustang, and nurse a hangover at a buddies' grave. It's going to be raining and he's going to be sad. Bet on it.

Cowboys are supposed to suffer. That's how they got complexions like discarded horseshoes, and why they hang out in dark bars with ceilings papered in cards, dollar bills, baseball caps, and bras. These guys have been rode hard and put away wet. They are missing fingers, teeth, and hair. They have cracked ribs, bad knees, and compression fractures. They, none of 'em, have health insurance.

Guys who wear chaps have never tasted a fresh-baked blueberry pie without falling in love with the girl who made it, prompting a lot of stories that will never get literary awards or appear on Salon.com. Cowboys are always clean-shaven and comfortable without electricity or plumbing. They don't put sunglasses on their dogs, frequent beaches, or drink margaritas. They were schooled in punching cows and hold graduate degrees in poking girls. They never read Walt Whitman, and they think Milton is the guy at the end of the bar.

Cowboys hold certain truths to be self-evident: country roads are always long and life is always short; October skies are always gray; outhouses are always cold and pickups are always old; range and trails are always open. The jailer's wife is always ugly and the girl next door is always the "purdyest thang" in the valley. You are what you smoke and you're gonna live till you die. "Home on the Range" is their national anthem. Right is right and wrong is wrong, and that, my friend, is the Code of the West.

Cowboys are always thinking and writing about the things that get them down: old age, Old Walleye, the view from the rearview mirror, working for someone else's brand, thin bedrolls, camp cooks, and foolish pride. They fantasize about their dogs and when they'll return to the home place. They dream about the last time they got throwed, and the next time they'll get throwed. They only think about pushing cows to grass, chasing cows through brush, and shipping cows for a fair price. They worry about crossing the Great Divide, dead-end roads, and whether Jesus was a cowboy.

These are not the problems that plagued Socrates, but thinking about them sure can make you laugh till your ribs hurt, and that's a blessing in January.

Their Horses

THE BOND BETWEEN a man and his horse is the most passionate love affair in history. It's more intense than man's affection for his best friend, who may or may not be his dog, and his adoration of woman, who may or may not be his wife.

Slim, who spends more time with his horse than his Old Lady, says his spouse could take a few lessons from his horse. Old Paint doesn't have headaches, talk back, expect sex, make lists of honey-do's, want flowers on her birthday, or whine when he's late. She doesn't smoke or eat crackers in bed. She doesn't shop, and two pair of shoes will do 'er. She can't sue you for alimony, although, face it, she can dump you on your ass and leave you high and dry.

Your horse, on the other hand, doesn't care whether you chew, sleep in your long johns, or need a shave. Whether you won him in a poker game, adopted him at a wild horse roundup, or bought him at a neighboring ranch, his love is unconditional. Regardless of breed, color, or age, he will clear the creek, maneuver the prairie dog town and, as Old Timers philosophize, turn on a quarter and give you fifteen cents change.

He doesn't give a damn whether you lost the tractor payment in a poker game or have a hole in your muffler. He is not impressed by the fact that you can do the crossword puzzle with a fountain pen. He'll never fault you for missing a Saturday night bath, because you smell just like him, and he'll always take you home, even when you're falling-down drunk. There's no better place to celebrate this special kinship than over a brew at the Stockyard Inn and Saloon during the National Western Stock Show.

Every January for one hundred years, guys in worn hats have made the pilgrimage to swap stories about the faithful nags that drag them up to hunting camp, off to mend fence, down to rodeo, out to round 'em up and head 'em out. They'll be bending elbows and ears with tales of wars against ticks, grasshoppers, prairie fires, drought, horse-flies, and quicksand. The stories are all more or less true and, if they aren't, they should be.

Let's face it, horses are everything men wanna be: smart, obedient, reliable, loving, self-sufficient, and hardworking. They never sit down on the job. They don't care if you're wearing a white hat or a black one, vote liberal or reactionary, play preacher or embezzler. They're simply grateful that you show up, throw 'em some hay and an occasional bucket of grain.

Like men, horses never ask for directions. And both are seeking greener pastures. Men, on the other hand, like conflict. It's a testosterone kind of thing. Ya gotta be at war with a bronc, a wayward cow, the elements, or the bastard on the other side of the road. Even if you aren't, it gives you something to grouse about.

Your horse may be a churn-head, cold-jawed salty, but he is loved—maybe because you don't have to yell at him, or maybe because you do. Big Bob had a team and a teetotaling Old Lady who frowned on cussing, so he named his plow horses Sonofabitch and Goddamn. It was the only way he could talk the way he wanted to within earshot of his wife, and you could hear him yelling at those plugs clear across the Divide.

The affection between man and mount is reflected in the 28,050 items involving horses on eBay: tie tacks, music boxes, bookends, racing programs, stamp collections, light switch covers, lamps, and shoehorns. Horses decorate earrings—running, bucking, cutting, roping, and nuzzling. They are featured on English Royal Doulton and Han dynasty vases. It's amazing how many people collect White Horse whiskey bottles, Barbie and her 1983 Arabian, pictures of Lady Godiva, and rocking horses that make "horsy sounds."

For the rancher who has everything, the internet provides cyber-shops that will put your horse's face on a mousepad for $8.99, and "cyberstables" that will profile him for $600 a year. A cybermuseum exhibits horse fossils found on a "sedimental journey" through the past 55 million years, and a museum at the University of Kansas proudly displays a real stuffed horse, Comanche, lone survivor of Custer's Last Stand at Little Big Horn.

Horses are revered in clothes, accessories, home décor, and toys. They are the focus of awards, competitions, festivals, races, shows, and clinics. Their legacy is documented in halls of fame, associations, clubs, appreciation days, magazines, libraries, catalogs, and directories. They are protected by rest homes, adoption services, defense funds, sanctuaries, and humane leagues.

Seems to be a continuing relationship. One of my favorite cowboys has been running cows five generations now. "You'd a-thought I wudda caught 'em by now," he says, and his horse just neighs.

Their Garages

MEN WHO HAVE GARAGES don't have affairs. They lust for automatic door openers, not sex. They dream about an additional bay, not weekends in Paris. Nothing compares to the peace and purpose a man can find in his garage, regardless of size, location, or number of doors. It doesn't matter how he votes, where he works, or what his age or income is. Every man wants a garage, preferably one with a recliner, TV, stereo, VCR, and fridge full of Budweiser. Check it out: the bigger the garage, the better the marriage.

The only reason men leave their garages is to go fishing or to a ball game, although some can be lured out to coach Little League, see a Rambo flick, or attend a tractor pull. They'll let the wife remodel the kitchen *only* because they can steal the old cabinets for the garage. They'll swear the lounger is broken so it can be retired to the garage. They can go without Viagra for weeks, but they cannot leave the garage for more than a few days.

Women retreat to the kitchen. Children are sent to their rooms. Men don't have to be banished to the garage because it's the place they most want to be. It offers the kind of exhilaration known only to those who live beyond the reach of nagging wives, know-it-all neighbors, and kids who whine. Everything needs room to grow, and husbands are no exception—they need their own space.

A man's home is not his castle, his garage is. There are few places on earth as intimate and comfortable. It's a sacred place where men can think, fart, and scratch crotch. It is a private place where they can play poker, grow pot, or make bombs. It's where they can laugh at a buddy's dirty jokes or cry when the garbage truck runs over the dog. It's where they can talk shop, track mud, leave things on the floor, and write phone numbers on the wall. It is where they are free to drink beer and waste time. Everything in it can be cleaned with Goof Off or kitty litter.

The garage is where men hang out without anyone chipping on them—where they can bullshit with the boys and get away with doing things they wouldn't dream of doing in the house, like pee in the drain. Where they store treasure: wing nuts, soldering irons, wiper blades, dead batteries, tires, hoses, belts, and filters. Where they archive expired license plates and hazardous waste, rusted nails and burned-out light bulbs, tubes without labels and empty paint cans. Where they can watch scraps of wood petrify.

Men evolved quickly from womb to cave, to lodge, to garage. Today's caveman needs a "Taj Magarage" big enough for a jeep, truck, motorcycle, van, Winnebago, ATV, and a motorboat. His dream house is a six-car garage attached to a bedroom and bath. Houses designed by men have miniscule bedrooms, kitchens, and baths, but mammoth garages. The garage dwarfs the lot, the garden, and the barn, and requires even more hosing out. Women can put things in closets and know exactly where they are. Men, on the other hand, need stuff in full sight, preferably where they can trip over it. That's why the garage was invented.

Think about it: Michelangelo had to have a place to store his paint cans. Ben Franklin needed somewhere to stash his kites. Pre-historic man needed a mini-cave to hide arrowheads and bones, and Bill Gates needed somewhere to invent Microsoft. If Newton had been hanging out in a garage, a box of old tax returns, not an apple, would have fallen on his head. Have you ever seen a happier guy than Tim-the-Tool-Man? He has a garage full of things with motors: air compressors, welders, and chain saws.

The garage is a place to hide stuff the Old Lady asked him to throw away. It is a home for kitchen sinks, lawnmowers, chainsaws, and broken furniture. It warehouses dreams: the canoe he's going to take to the lake when it's patched, a muffler for a Porsche he'll never own, the bathtub for a house he wants to build. There's a pump he's going to repair for the hundred-year flood, and a crib he's refinishing for his first great-grandchild.

The garage is not just a place, it's a state of mind. It is the symbol of life without doilies, Day-Timers, and closet organizers. It's where no one tells him where to put the hammer, and even if it's buried under the ragbag, he knows exactly where it is. Unlike a bar or bedroom, it's the place where he is in control. The remote gives him absolute power over the door, something he never has over the wife. Only wimps outline their tools on pegboard—real men always know where they left the ratchet.

Houses are feminine. Garages are masculine. It's spelled out in the Emancipation Proclamation, the Bill of Rights and the pre-nups. She gets the house and he gets the garage. Some guys pick their friends by the size of their garage. Garages have more status than carports or sheds. Men with "Taj Magarages" have lots of testosterone. Not every man wants to be a millionaire, but every man wants a garage.

On Community

Paying Your Dues

IN A SMALL TOWN it is incumbent upon newcomers to observe the ritual of "joining" something, anything, to prove the sincerity of their interest in "giving back to the community." The last one over the Pass is required to go a little slower, show a little respect, refrain from suggesting that they did it better in wherever they came from, especially Texas.

This includes, but is not limited to, baking brownies, selling raffle tickets, and ushering at a gazillion events you have no desire to attend. Frequently it requires you to open your house for the Lions Club Garden Tour, babysit the senior citizens center art exhibit, or organize a citywide garage sale. Inevitably, it involves a series of meetings that will, on more than one occasion, force you to miss supper, cancel a dentist appointment, and be late for work.

"Becoming involved" is an art form. It includes joining at least one tax-exempt, do-good organization, preferably the arts council, quilting club, or hospital auxiliary because there is no way you can run for the school board or planning commission until you have "paid your dues." On the Fast Track, you sign up for the historic preservation committee, League of Women Voters, or library board. Pluggers stick with the Rotary, quilters, and the bowling league.

The Board of Adjustment doesn't provide the proper grooming for a spread in the *Lifestyles* section of the local rag. Political and religious organizations are equally taboo, a dead end on the road to Hubba Hubba, the world of Slide and Glide. The ultimate success is being asked to chair the annual United Way campaign.

But then there was Sonia. Sonia went to great lengths to avoid the economic, social, and political drudgery of community involvement. She detested meetings. She had no interest in reviewing the minutes of the last gathering and no patience for arranging the carpool to the next. Barbara's peanut brittle, which seemed to be served at every one of them, held no appeal.

Sonia became "involved" by marrying the biggest, richest developer in town. She said she was looking for a Sugar Daddy when she arrived from San Antonio, and she landed him just months after his divorce. At his suggestion, she dyed her hair red and got breast implants because he liked having a "looker" to squire about town. She liked having a fleet of housekeepers, caterers, and gardeners on call. They relieved her of nasty, time-consuming chores like making supper and washing socks. So Sonia had plenty of time to ride her horse, hunt chanterelles, and think about how to make the town a better place to live.

Sonia lived in a three-story Victorian on the big hill above town, affectionately known as "Snob Knob." She was smart, beautiful, and rich, which made no nevermind to the Boys in the Bar until she somehow got appointed to the planning commission. No one could figure how it happened because she certainly hadn't "paid her dues" and no one would 'fess up to nominating her. It only began to matter when she started allowing meetings to drag past midnight while she munched on Reese's Pieces. The Old Men grumbled because they had to get up early to feed cows, and their Old Ladies hated the fact the she could consume so much chocolate without gaining weight.

Sonia was quick to find a "cause" to champion: a bond issue for a bike path that would greenbelt her house. She abandoned yoga lessons to chair the feasibility committee and postponed a trip to Paris to chair the Friends of the Big, Bigger, Biggest Bike Path Committee. She was charming at Lions, Kiwanis, and Rotary. She chatted up the PEO, the Book Club, and the Auxiliary. She lunched with the League of Women Voters, shared potluck with the AAUW, and dunked donuts with the Old Ladies at assisted living.

Sonia made the case eloquently. She talked about our environment and the need to save it, our river and the need to preserve it, our trails lined with serviceberries and the need to can them. Our athletes, seniors, and dogs, and the need to exercise them. Our tourists and the growing need to entertain them. She divided the miles of bike path by the mill levy increase, and she calculated the impact of every one of those proposed miles upon the economy of the town. She described how they do it in Texas.

The bond issue passed. No one could figure out how it happened because Sonia had never ushered at a band concert, baked cookies for the PTA Open House, or sold a raffle ticket for the museum expansion.

School Bonds

THERE IS NOTHING that tears a town apart faster than a school bond election. It pits mothers against daughters, husbands against wives. Last week my neighbor said she didn't know if we could be friends any more. Another called to share her disgust at finding me in agreement with "those dirt bags at 11th and Pine." I caught Marie walking her dog after dark to avoid visiting with anyone on the path. Jane started sending her kid to the grocery store, and Cheryl stopped attending committee meetings.

Connie's still incensed about the time a former superintendent of schools pulled his boat to the edge of Lake Powell with the school district's van and forgot to put the brakes on, so it rolled. The van sank but his boat, of course, floated. She simply won't forgive and forget. And she refuses to speak to her neighbor, a veteran of 842 years on the school board, who claims that because no one came to the school board meetings to object to the master plan, they assumed they were "doing it right."

We all live in communities that spend a lot of time and energy building partnerships, coalitions, and networks whose sole purpose is to plan, vision, and collaborate. Then along comes the bond issue, and poof, it's over. We are at each other's throats, exhibiting speech and behavior patterns unacceptable in the preschool green room. The Head Start program was founded to prevent the kind of behavior exhibited at the public debates.

Committees form and dissolve in the night. It is impossible to tell which is pro or con. Parents, Teachers, and Citizens for Better Education and Management deliver the flyers. Citizens for Even More Better Schools take out a full-page ad. Expense and rancor are directly related to the millions of dollars involved. The millions involved are directly related to the number of public statements from bank presidents and civic leaders. Bank presidents like bond issues because they get interest on the notes, and civic leaders like them because they are the bank presidents.

School bond elections are tough on everyone: the young are too poor to pay for it and seniors don't have children in school. Some claim it's a bare-bones proposal while others say the proposed building looks like the Waldorf Astoria. Some argue that we've got to start somewhere while others demand more study. There are those who think you can raise $45 million at bake sales. Others are convinced that we can come up with a better plan, despite the fact that no one has in twenty-five years.

It doesn't matter when the issue comes up or where you live, there are reasons to vote *for* the bond issue, and reasons to vote *against* the bond issue. Tack this list on the refrigerator door because, with minor editing, the arguments can be applied to future debates over bond issues for water treatment plants, libraries, or hospital districts. It will be particularly handy next year when, after failing by 117 votes, the bond issue will rise from the ashes, be revisited, reduced, and passed unanimously.

On the one hand we owe it to our children. On the other, the old building was good enough for my grandpa so it's good enough for my kids.

On the one hand buildings don't educate children. On the other, the roof leaks.

On the one hand you want to use the money to pay teachers. On the other, that's illegal.

On the one hand the school board has studied long and hard and is convinced this is the very best plan. On the other, no one trusts the school board with a $2 bill.

On the one hand the levy only costs pennies. On the other, it's enough to send a kid to college when spread over the life of the bond issue.

On the one hand the planning department swears by its enrollment growth projections. On the other, planning departments always do and are consistently wrong.

On the one hand families moving into town can share the cost of growth, decreasing the burden on long-time residents. On the other, Mildred James was a lousy teacher when I was in school so she certainly doesn't deserve a new classroom.

On the one hand it's cheaper than the bond issue passed by (fill in the name of a comparable community). On the other, we don't want to be anything like (repeat name of town).

On the one hand interest rates will never be lower and we have a watchdog committee to assure there will be no cost overruns. On the other, you might want to buy the Brooklyn Bridge.

Culture Mavens

UP AT DRY LAKE, where we still blot our lipstick and file our nails in public, we subscribe to the theory that art is in the eye of the beholder and, therefore, includes Selma's portraits of clowns on velveteen. So no one was surprised when Clara won a blue ribbon in mixed media at the county fair for a perfectly symmetrical, beautifully textured, elegantly framed dried cowpie. In fact, Maggie's earthy landscapes, complete with elk and sage brush, are realistic precisely because she paints them in oils mixed with soil—sand from the Red Desert, mud from Mesa Mountain, and dirt from up Fortification Creek. The fact that she promotes them as "dirty pictures" is not only accurate but popular with the Boys at the Bar, where Cowboy Culture still rules.

This down 'n' dirty attitude really rankles the Culture Mavens who have moved here from Chicago, L.A., or New York with a lot of baggage: looks, brains, and attitude. They have all the answers and feel compelled to share them with soccer moms, the library board, and the League of Women Voters. They know *Robert's Rules of Order* and Julia Child's recipe for escargot. They buy their jeans from J. Jill and read *The New Yorker*. With absolutely no prompting they will tell you how to throw a better bake sale or pass a bigger bond issue, because "everything was done better" in Chicago, L.A., New York, or wherever it was they came from.

Despite the fact that they just came over the Pass ten minutes ago, Culture Mavens are violently loyal to the town's vision, image, and bond ratings. They take themselves very seriously and, even those without children, husbands, or jobs, seem to relish being "stressed," although they have ample time for yoga, facials, and endless meetings of the arts council. They live on thirty-five-acre "ranches," log houses and no dogs, stainless steel kitchens and no children. They decorate with coyotes and cowboy hats, and dress their couches up in leather.

Culture Mavens may not be able to define what art is, but they know good art when they see it, and they can toss the word "oeuvre" into any discussion. Some have been to Seattle to examine Art in Public Places. Others make periodic pilgrimages to the Metropolitan and the Getty. Most have lunched at museums of modern art in towns east of the Mississippi. They know the difference between Mama and MOMA, mauve and puce, and they all hate Robert Mapplethorpe.

Culture Mavens know that "good art" is never controversial and that it always matches your sofa. They love meeting in the city council chambers where they can swivel around in the high-backed chairs and glare down at the less couth over designer spectacles. But, mostly, they worry about running out of toilet paper at the arts center and the lifestyle of the sixth-grade band teacher.

No one is better equipped to manage the artistic life of our town. One is teaching fudge-fingered kids how to play the piano while their mothers lounge outside in air-conditioned SUVs, smoking and reading Danielle Steele. Others stay *au courant* by throwing pots in the ceramics studio, acting in community theatre, or simply writing checks to the arts center. The former wife of the former mayor remains involved with the arts by coordinating the color of her eyeshadow with the season, brown for fall and blue for spring. Cynthia serves as chair because her nephew went to Julliard.

Down at the Corral Club, the Boys at the Bar do not feel compelled to invest time or tax dollars in efforts to prove that our town is really-o-truly-o committed to the arts. They knew that putting a bust of William Wordsworth in the downtown park wasn't going to fly with Old Jake's widow, the mayor's wife who donated the land for the park dedicated to her husband. The piece had to be removed, she insisted, because Jake was more of a Robert Service kind of a guy.

Budget Busters

IF THE COLOR of money is green, why is the bottom line always red? Why can't the greening of America involve cash? Americans are adventurous, innovative, and gutsy. We are survivors. We can live off the land, build with duct tape, and fix anything with string. We crossed the plains with oxen and landed on the moon with Styrofoam tiles. We have weathered depression, war, and terrorism. Why, then, do we have so much trouble balancing a budget?

Come spring, budget busters at city halls, county seats, school boards, special districts, and nonprofit organizations are hustling to balance the books prior to opening day of the Fiscal Year, funded or unfunded. To their dismay, the chasm between revenues and expenditures cannot be plugged with Visa cards.

Whenever the federales can't balance the books, they just mandate that the states pick up the cost of their Beltway solutions for the Hinterlands. Over in the grasslands some legislators are thinking that selling the Kansas turnpike would be a swell way to raise money for that state's empty coffers without increasing taxes. But the governor assures that she has no intention of privatizing the 236-mile strip, even if some Think Tank has valued it at $900 million.

The Boys at the Bar, whose political sensitivities and personal ethics are substantially enhanced by another round, say they sure-as-hell know how to balance a budget: keep a second set of books, quit paying your income tax, don't pay withholding, and transfer the cost of maintaining computers and copiers to the capital equipment fund because they're equipment, aren't they? The trouble began, they'll tell you, when the Powers That Be couldn't decide whether the first of the year was July 1, October 1, or January 1.

Betsy-the-Beautician simply charges her long distance calls to the local bank. Marv-the-Nailjockey writes short checks. He just tears off one end so anyone with half a brain can tell it is short. Of course, every few months some snippy bank teller confiscates his checkbook until he makes good on his bar tabs all over town. He died owing the local liquor store seven grand.

Book Clubs

THE LOSERS' BOOK CLUB is a monthly gathering of overeducated, overworked, and overhormoned ladies, firm in the conviction that no one has ever written a book that couldn't be improved upon by eating chocolate. Regardless of the fact that the decibel level during the chew-and-chat drowns out the junior high school band, the Losers' Book Club attracts the best and the brightest.

It is open to everyone who has lost an election, lover, library card, or the car keys. It embraces the harried masses of Loser Ladies who have lost their place in a book, their place in line, their marriages, cars in parking lots, tickets to the theater, or an election. Some have never been invited to join a book club and others have been thrown out of them. "Cliffies," ladies who got through school on Cliff Notes, are especially welcome.

The Losers' Book Club started shortly after Marjean turned the uptown book club into a literary pressure cooker by suggesting that Clara was dumber'n dirt because she liked *The Sweet Potato Queens' Book of Love*, to say nothing of the fact that she made the world's worst rum balls. The ladies were lounging around her heart-shaped swimming pool, munching on catered tidbits and discussing which absent members were touring Europe that month, when Marjean pointed out that it didn't matter what book they were going to read next month because Clara had not been voted into membership.

That's when Clara began the search for a suitable book club. The first one she tried shut down after Margaret Jane got shit-faced and attacked everyone who failed to savor the symbolism, classicism, and significance of *Cold Mountain*. The Blue Hairs' Book Club, twenty-seven English professors who wallowed in every detail of every classic, especially *Moby Dick*, truly enjoyed quizzing each other on who was where, doing what, when whatever was said to whom. Clara lasted until they decided, with gusto, to assign the *Iliad* for summer reading.

So Clara and a gaggle of girl friends, Losers all, organized the ultimate Losers' Book Club. Harriet qualified because she was not appointed to a second term on the planning commission. Beth's husband left her and three children for a twenty-five-year-old bimbo. Nancy dropped out of Weight Watchers. And every last one of 'em relished getting out of the house for an occasional cocktail with the girls.

The Losers' Book Club is governed, albeit loosely, by a few "rules" developed over a little glass of wine, in order to prevent Rita from holding forth on vaginal dryness, her topic du jour every jour. Standing committees are appointed to watchdog party favors, morals, whining, decorum, and the meaning of life. The ever-pending school bond election is always off limits.

Criteria for membership in the Losers' Book Club requires that you read in the bathtub, enjoy books on tape, move your lips while reading, or have harbored a book unopened on the nightstand for more than a year. It is preferred, but not mandatory, that you loved *The Education of Little Tree*, hated *Snow Falling on Cedars*, and lied about having read *Ivanhoe* in eighth grade. No one gives a damn whether you read *Cosmo*, ballot issues, or nutritional labels, and it matters not that you can't name a single Sidney Sheldon title.

There are three items on every agenda: shoot-the-shit, serious discussion, and show-and-share. Shoot-the-shit includes, but is not limited to, gossip, malicious and otherwise. Show-and-share is a meaningful consideration of social, philosophical, economic, or political issues prompted by literature or life.

The bylaws are designed to, but cannot assure, that we sometimes, but not always, turn our attention to serious discussion. Rita allowed as how she can live with the bylaws:

(1) We will read books both great and small.
(2) You need not read the book to attend.
(3) We will meet damn near monthly.
(4) Guests are welcome.
(5) Books must be paperback and available at the supermarket.
(6) There will be no books on self-help, therapy, or do-gooding.

(7) Soccer Moms are welcome as long as they do not participate in the discussion.
(8) Mention of medical problems, husbands, or children is a punishable offense.
(9) Martha Stewart need not sanction the refreshments.
(10) Drinking is not only allowed, but recommended.

Potluck Suppers

IN THE COLORADO OUTBACK, where we are born knowing how to make Divinity and date balls, summer ushers in a social season defined by potluck suppers. Anna Nicole Smith and Courtney Love don't go to potluck suppers, but I do and I'm here to tell ya that you can get brain damage from eating too much tuna fish casserole with fried onions on top.

Maybe that's why no one seems to know the origins of the word "potluck." Some claim it comes from the Irish, who like to prepare dinner in a single pot, or the French, who simmer leftovers on the back of the stove in a pottage. Others claim it dates from 1592 when settlers began to swap recipes with native people for whom "pot-latch" meant sharing.

Today, potluck suppers define America. They are the gustatorial equivalent of a barn raising. Whether you call them a bake, a feed, a fry, a cook-off, or a covered-dish supper, they symbolize community because everyone participates, contributes, and overindulges. This is particularly true if Selma serves her Key Lime Surprise.

Potlucks are as American as apple pie, which is always featured, along with hamburgers, hot dogs, slaw, beans, and other national delicacies that Eleanor Roosevelt served to the king and queen of England, who were not on Weight Watchers at the time.

Recently, when bureaucrats in Illinois and Washington discovered that those states had laws requiring establishments serving food to hire certified food handlers, the nation was threatened at its core. Legislatures and governors acted quickly to protect liberty, justice, and the freedom to indulge in Mavis's pecan pie.

Fortunately, the Colorado Food Service Code has always exempted cuisine for families and fundraisers served at public gatherings from regulations requiring hairnets. A blessing it is, too, because without potlucks, church basements, school gyms, and community centers would stand empty. The Book Club might be spared more of Madge's meatloaf.

Potlucks are the purview of people who use paper plates and drink canned pop at the dinner table, people who have been dancing with the same partner for forty-seven years. They are organized by women who use hair spray and relished by men who sharpen pencils with pocket knives. They attract people who eat out at the Dairy Queen and take pride in the fact that they have nine children, all of whom live within a twenty-mile radius. Without exception, they cook beef and green beans long enough to be sure they're dead, and they never eat seafood, not even deep-fat fried.

Up at Dry Lake we are forever searching yard sales for hot pads that look like barnyard animals, and chintz and wicker cozies for casserole dishes. Our kitchen towels are checkered and the cords on our hot plates are scorched. We decorate our homes in Early Duck, use checkered tablecloths, and share even our most cherished pasta recipes on filing cards decorated with sweet peas. We are the people who keep Pyrex in business because it's impossible to remember to write your name on the bottom of every dish you're going to abandon at the community center.

The word "potluck" is synonymous with "homestyle," a euphemism for high cholesterol, high fat, and a high chance of requiring an antacid. The ingredients can always be found at the supermarket, prepared in nineteen minutes, and will, more'n likely, involve Miracle Whip in summer and Cool Whip in winter. Dishes can be served in the ugly casseroles you received as wedding presents, and are, more often than not, white. Mavis's creamed chicken on top of noodles, on top of mashed potatoes, took this year's prize for comfort, cholesterol, and calories.

Dry Lake has a population of 317 but even more recipes for rhubarb pie. How to crimp the crust has been Topic A for generations of ladies in church basements throughout the county. Every one of 'em knows what to do with cream of tartar, how to scald milk, and how to cook with Karo syrup. They all use gingersnaps as seasoning.

Although Emeril Lagasse and thousands of ministers' wives have written potluck cookbooks, not one of them recommends the appropriate wine to accompany any of the three million potluck recipes on the web. I plan to address this omission in my forthcoming book, *101 Uses for Chicken-Fried Steak*, which will include "A History of Peanut Brittle" and a "North American Field Guide to Pie Socials." It will also share my secret recipe for Sauerkraut Surprise Cake, a family favorite that, in the interest of controlling national health care costs, best remains secret.

Planners

I AM SICK of partnerships, coalitions, and collaborations. I am tired of bold, imaginative new ideas. I am exhausted by strategic planning. I don't want to revisit the mission statement, re-examine resources, or redefine the quality of life. I don't want to be a stakeholder, a facilitator, a decision maker, or a community leader. I don't want to be empowered. I would rather have a health club membership.

I am sick of sitting in the church basement trying to update the comprehensive plan, problem-solve, and vision. I am tired of the hunt for benchmarks, key indicators, initiatives, indices, trends, leverage points, themes, and performance areas. Hannibal got over the Alps without them. Lewis and Clark opened the West without them. And we can probably build a sewage treatment plant at Dry Lake without them.

But we remain enchanted with the process. We are obsessed with goals, objectives, and action plans. The Boys at the Bar say no amount of focusing by focus groups will landscape the median west of town, fire the school superintendent, or repair the Meals-on-Wheels van. The city council is going to do whatever it damn well pleases, regardless of what the planning commission recommends. The chamber of commerce will continue to promote the town, no matter how many bumper stickers beg them to stop the brutal marketing. The school board is going full-speed ahead with a mega-million-dollar bond issue that no one in town, not even the teachers, supports.

Crazydave-the-Plumber says the simple truth is the stuff what needs doing isn't gonna get done by gabbing. You can jawbone till you're blue in the face, but you can't round 'em up and head 'em out until someone gets in the saddle. It only takes eight seconds to make the bell, he says, so how long can it take to decide where to put the new crapper in city park, whether to pave County Road 6, or who should buy the next round?

The Boys at the Bar don't hold much truck with consultants, study groups, and consensus building. They say you can bring a town to its knees by proposing to mall the main drag, expand the water treatment plant, issue a tax abatement, or remodel city hall. You can knot up local government for years by suggesting that the highway bypass town, that school districts be unified, or that the city and county consolidate communication systems, recreation districts, or fire and ambulance services. You can blow a perfectly good fishing day or a lifetime worrying about whether or not we need a comprehensive plan or a bike path, an environmental needs assessment or a stop light.

They say there are more effective ways to make a point: throw a Boston cream pie at the city manager; storm the meeting; send a dead skunk to your county commissioner; write a scathing letter to the editor; paper the courthouse lawn; hang the mayor in effigy.

The Boys at the Bar only had to march on the courthouse once. It was their constitutional duty, they said, to tell the county commissioners, loud and clear, that they were totally out of line. The town's real infrastructure, a dozen or so Good Ol' Boys, just appeared at the commission's Tuesday morning Q&A, hats on, legs bowed, Red Dog stuffed in the lower lip. They lined out right on the front bench— the vet, the owner of the hardware store, the manager of the co-op, the barkeep at the Corral Club—to tell the commissioners how it was going to be.

No matter how many peer reviews, steering committees, or quality controls the county could muster, the arts council was not going to put a sixteen-foot-high cement cowboy hat on the courthouse lawn. They didn't care if the Culture Mavens said it represented our western heritage, or whether it was made by some la-de-da big city artist from the East. It made no nevermind that the Economic Gardeners said it would promote tourism. It cut no ice that the extension agent's wife chaired the site committee. They didn't give a rat's ass how important Art in Public Places was to the chamber, the valley, and the future of civilization.

The artsy-fartsies could take their Art in Public Places out to the mall or down to the bike path. The shooting range and the dump were suggested. But the courthouse lawn, like the rodeo grounds, was to be reserved for the true icons of our heritage, Colorado blue spruce and the church roster. An exception might be made for a picnic table or two, but not for art. The Boys at the Bar prevailed, of course, because that's how planning works up at Dry Lake.

Life in Eventsville

THE WEST HAS ALWAYS been about selling postcard memories. Still is. Once upon a time we ventured west to build campfires and spin a tale or two. Today we come seeking front row seats at chamber music festivals.

Brutal marketing changes landscapes and lifestyles. Friday night jackpot rodeo has gone pro. Square dances have turned into wine tastings. Alpine meadows have been abandoned for cement Alpine slides, and the only Mustang roundups are staged on the main drag so tourists can gawk at vintage cars.

My town is obsessed with tournaments, fairs, hoedowns, and competitions. We are hell-bent on becoming the Events Capital of the World. You gotta wonder what makes towns go to such amazing lengths to attract tourists when the locals aren't going to do anything but grouse about the lack of parking downtown and the need for help from Search and Rescue to maneuver I-70. Where was it determined that triathlons and hot air balloon races are the only way to get listed in full-color tourist guides? Who decided that we all want to live in Neverland?

Fact is, I don't want to be entertained, stimulated, and intrigued 24/7. I do not feel compelled to stuff my leisure with pie-eating contests, zucchini bake-offs, and rhubarb festivals. I don't want to spend my weekends watching monster truck climbs, tractor pulls, and pig wrestling. I'm tired of races, whether stock cars, beds, burros, or balloons. I'm not up for plate-smashing, cornhusking, or beer-guzzling contests.

There aren't enough microbrews in America to make me care whether the cops or the firefighters win a tug of war. I really hate corn dogs, turkey legs, and cotton candy. I just want to be somewhere where Michael Martin Murphy is not playing, but my dog can.

It used to be that the town hosted a Cleanup Day, a Farmers' Market, and some band concerts in the park. Period. We spent a lot of time skipping rocks in the river and watching the sun come up and go down. We hunted serviceberries along unpaved roads, poked the fire and stared into space. Old Ladies made pepper relish while their Old Men sat on the porch swatting flies. Kids did chores in the morning and spent the afternoons blowing fuzzy heads off dandelions.

Conversation was an activity, and wasting time was an art form. Our lives were not enhanced by wearing fringe, alligator boots, and $19.95 cowboy hats, and preparation for the county fair consumed a huge chunk of the year. We didn't drink stuff to replenish electrolytes, sodium, and potassium, and we never gave much thought to whether a day called for 30 or 90 SPF. No one had heard of righteous chi.

Personally, I've had my fill of craft shows, art fairs, and garden tours. I'm sick of music and film festivals. I don't want to attend another gala, fashion show, or benefit. I'm calling it quits on anything requiring silly hats and buckets of cash. No more fundraisers to save shoeless kids and starving horses, or vice versa. No more karaoke contests, chili cook-offs, retreats, or reenactments. No more art shows, juried or not.

It's all I can do to remember, much less celebrate, family birthdays and anniversaries, much less national holidays. I don't need any more merriment on my "to do" list. There is no room on the refrigerator door for more reminders to take brownies to the potluck, snacks to the game, and pop to the picnic.

While the last ones over the Pass are downtown wallowing in special events, locals are hiding in the woods, chasing chanterelles and fiddle ferns. They don't want to bet on another Turkey Drop or toss another cowpie. They have tired of festivals celebrating peaches, strawberries, and mushrooms. They don't need to win another gold buckle, gold nugget, or stuffed moose.

So much activity just makes me want to sit under a tree with Ferdinand the Bull and smell the flowers. But, before retiring to the woods, I plan to check out the Great Fruitcake Toss at Manitou Springs, the Tick Festival in Heeney, and the Outhouse Tour over in North Park.

Because, if the economic development gurus continue to have their way, every frontier town in Colorado will soon be hosting an NFL team, polo matches, and regattas for visitors jetting into their duty-free airports. Somewhere, right this minute, someone is thinking about building a Mall of the Rockies behind the courthouse and a Six Flags theme park out by the gravel pit. You can bet on it.

On Holidays

Granny's Commencement Address

I WANT TO GIVE a commencement address. I want to stand in front of an auditorium full of beaming youngsters and boomer parents and pontificate on the monumental truths I have gleaned being rode hard and put away wet. I don't much care whether the speech is to elementary school, high school, or college graduates. My message would be the same: Grow up to be cowboys.

Cowboys say please, thank you, and ma'am. They help old ladies across the street and keep their mouths shut and their eyes open. They spend their time fixing things that are broke instead of analyzing political, religious, or birth-control preferences, yours or theirs. They live free of mission statements, leadership conferences, and personal coaches. And they always get back on the horse.

Given the opportunity, I would urge young graduates to keep the myth of the Wild West alive. Lie some, laugh often, and love lots. Write bad poems and good letters to the editor. Sing outside the shower. Watch prairie chickens dance. Summit all fifty-four fourteeners. Drive a vehicle with a crash bar and tow-ball mount. Jeep every dirt road in the county and cut a few new ones. Have the gumption to live out your dreams.

Boys, find a good horse, a good dog, and a good woman. Nail the Hartford elk. Fall off a bucking horse and win a fence line dispute. Make friends who can fix parking tickets and get your kid his first job.

Girls, kiss enough frogs to locate a prince. Use the good china everyday. Drink wine only in corked bottles. Stay good-looking, good-hearted, and good-humored, and buy red satin nighties.

Learn to play the fiddle, in-line skate, and make cappuccino. If you never have the opportunity to make love on top of a bar, at least dance on top of one. Seek only green pastures and clear mountain lakes. Light up meadows with your smile, and laugh loud enough to rattle windows in the next county. If you must go to symphonies, have the decency to stay awake. If you insist upon serving on the hospital board, be good enough to make a hefty contribution to their capital campaign. Don't ever take a job that requires a hairnet, and quit any job when the canary stops singing.

Think about careers you know nothing about: maybe become an extension agent. Astonish the world (and your mother) with a spectacular invention: a jet-powered snowboard, maybe. Explore places whose names you can't spell: Rarotonga comes to mind. Read books your teachers never assigned, or better yet, write one. Dress up for Halloween and go trick-or-treating for scotch. Use a little imagination—don't paint by the numbers.

Be a scoundrel. Spend sunup so you have stories to tell at sundown. Plan ahead—make sure that seventy years from now, when you're hanging out in a rocker taking your Coors through a straw, you have something to remember. Don't get carted off to the nursing home with nothing on your mind, no memories, no complaints. Be a curmudgeon.

Go somewhere, be somebody, and *do* something besides lunch. Don't sleep with the mailman. Don't slander the mayor. Don't shoot squirrels in front of kids, and, for goodness sake, don't admit to gunning down prairie dogs. In fact, it may be best to dummy up about the times you drained the beaver pond, put sugar in the English teacher's gas tank, poached a deer, and made love in the poison ivy.

Maybe skip the stories about stealing hubcaps, outhouses, and Christmas trees. Pretend you never scaled the fence to skinny dip in the city pool at midnight. Forget to mention getting a DUI on your dad's dozer. The world and the local gendarmerie are not now, and never will be, ready to embrace veterans of the weekly police blotter. But, more important, show a little tolerance when your kids get caught pulling the same capers for which you never got caught.

My pal Tyke-the-Carpenter is fond of pointing out that while some people lead good lives, others make life worth living. I say, go for quality. Grow flowers, ideas, and children. Walk tall, run fast, and range far. Put a $5,000 mountain bike on top of your $500 car and exceed the speed limit.

In the World According to Granny, you should all grow up to be cowboys, no matter where you live.

Granny's Marriage Counseling

THE KID NEXT DOOR is getting married next week. He found a beautiful girl with big brown eyes who shares his passion for climbing, biking, and kayaking. They finished college and signed up for the Peace Corps, which sits well with the mothers. They registered for wedding presents at Ace Hardware, to the delight of the fathers. They will be married on the banks of the Yampa River in bare feet, which was not what grandma had in mind.

This young couple found love exploring the beauty of the outdoors, prowling about the Grand Canyon, Yellowstone, and Yosemite. He says she baits her own hook. She says he extends her reach. Like the mountains and rivers of the West where they grew up, they were living wild and free until they had to plan a wedding.

Getting married is not easy. No matter how many guidebooks, websites, consultants, and planners are called into play, the father of the bride will make an endless toast and the mother of the groom is not going to shut up and wear beige. The dog will get into the hors d'oeuvres, and the children will sample the booze. Aunt Lena will pass out from the heat, the race for the bouquet can turn into a cat fight, and the best man might have to be roped to a tree until he sobers up.

Tying the knot is a risky business. I know from personal experience. I got married in a frontier town courthouse in a four-sentence ceremony witnessed by two fathers. The wedding party, which had been drinking in the parking lot while the judge mumbled words and shuffled papers, adjourned across the street to Vera's Bar and Grill and enjoyed a few more rounds. My father, already stressed from the rehearsal dinner, where the groom's Stetson was filled with champagne and passed around the table for toasts, was horrified. He had a heart attack and died the next day.

My pal Tony was a mama's boy. Mama never stopped packing his lunches, doing his laundry, and planning his schooling, jobs, and marriage. For more than two decades Mama held the reins so tight that, by the time Tony stood at the altar with a perfectly nice girl, he was in an extraordinary state of anxiety. He blacked out, passed out, and was hauled out of the church by paramedics. Tony finally escaped Mama in an ambulance trailed by the bride and six bridesmaids.

Turning life into a love letter is not easy. Never has been. Socrates and Hallmark had a lot to say on the subject but, let's face it, there is no operator's manual. Somebody's going to get locked out of the house, forget to take out the trash, and fail to pay the electric bill on time. She will eat crackers in bed. He will wash the lights with the darks. She will lose the keys to the car, and he will forget to feed the cat. They are going to disagree about how to put up the tent and how to poke the fire. You can bet on it.

Friends and family want them to plant flowers, prowl continents, sing in the shower, and remember to stop at children's lemonade stands. We want them to make love on the kitchen floor, drink champagne, and support each other and the communities in which they live. We will be there to remind them to call home and, no matter what the neighbors say, play the music loud.

We hope the homes they build will be full of books and music. That the children they raise will be surrounded with opportunity and affection. That their jobs will make some corner of the world a little better place in which to live. That they will bring laughter and meaning into the lives of their friends. That they will grow old sharing thoughts that do not have to be spoken, finishing each other's sentences, and falling in love with each other, over and over and over again.

This wedding is a romance fit for a Dick and Jane Reader, promising love, marriage, and baby carriages. This is not the time to dwell on the tuna fish casserole years for young marrieds, the macaroni and cheese years with kids, the barbecue years in the burbs, the sushi years in an empty nest, or the mashed potato years in a nursing home.

We'll ignore the years when Dick was sleeping on the couch and Jane was at her mother's. But, then again, they may get it right the first time.

Opening Day

IF YOU EVER PLAN to rob a bank in Colorado, do it on opening day of hunting season. That's when the sheriff and the police chief turn into outfitters, chauffeuring dudes around the outback on ATVs. Wives are at the mall "getting even" with the Old Man for neglecting them and the yard work. Girlfriends are at the beauty parlor getting gussied up to cook liver 'n' onions.

Men and boys are in the High Country where life is good because they can wear dirty underwear, forget about shaving, and fart in the bedroll. They are alone with their rifles, horses, and buddies, sharing warm beer and coffee laced with Maker's Mark. They are preparing to test themselves against the land and to inflict the details of that conquest upon anyone within earshot for the next sixty years.

Colorado residents celebrate the dawning of three holidays: Christmas, New Year's, and Elk Season. Opening day of hunting season is by far the most important. At our house it kicks off with Uncle Smokey's Thanksgiving Dinner Prayer: "Bless us, oh Lord, for these thy gifts, and for the elk which we are about to receive." Provisioning for hunting camp would put the Pilgrims to shame. Planning can occupy the entire year leading up to departure for the High Country, but swapping lies and laughter about the experience will fill a lifetime thereafter.

Opening day stories, like Aesop's Fables, get told and retold. Like moonshine, they improve with age. They are best shared at the Corral Club, the O-Aces, Stockman's, or someplace where the Old Lady isn't around to point out that it didn't really happen that way. They are particularly appropriate in the garage, where Cabela's catalogs are readily available for reference.

Lonny claims he ties his elk to a tree so he can bag him at dawn. Tyke remembers the time he got up to pee before first light and shot a seven-point from his bedroom window while still in his underwear.

The Paxton Brothers still brag on the day their family legally took six cows and a seven-point with bows, and were at the VFW eating eggs over easy by 7:30 A.M. Tex is still whining about the herd that sauntered into his backyard shortly after he packed off into the dark on a ten-mile hike to the side of the mountain the herd left.

Arleen is not about to let anyone forget the time she was in hunting camp, washing up breakfast grease, when she heard a shot and saw her horse go down. Of course she went berserk, shrieking obscenities and screaming, "You killed my horse!" into the surrounding woods. No sooner did her horse stand up, unharmed, than a six-point elk stumbled into camp and fell dead at her feet. Of course, no hunter in his right mind was about to walk into her fury, even to lay claim to that elk, so Arleen had her kill gutted and hung by the time her companions returned empty handed.

Crazydave-the-Plumber and Glen ran the sewer cleaning machine and hunted Swamp Park together for twenty years. They shared Smith & Wesson catalogs and hunting stories, so Crazydave felt bad when Glen had to check into the hospital for a hernia operation on the eve of opening day.

Crazydave went up to the hospital with a six-pack to wish Glen well and to remind him of the shot he missed because he was taking a leak. Glen wasn't about to let Crazydave forget the time he wet his pants when a buck spooked him from behind. No one was surprised when Glen, overcome by nostalgia, walked into hunting camp before dawn the next morning. He said he didn't have time to leave a note at the hospital explaining how's come his bed was empty. Opening day with the boys was clearly more important than a hernia, he said, maybe even more important than a Bronco game.

Not even a bank heist can disturb the calm that bathes the Rockies before the first opening day shot is fired. Alpenglow cannot compete with the orange glow generated by thousands of fleece-lined guys sitting on rocks, eating candy bars, and drinking antifreeze. Opening day is a sacred time that, more often than not, produces more stories than meat.

Kansas Is for the Birds

TEN THOUSAND SUVs leave Colorado for Kansas every November when bird hunting season opens. The Kansas Department of Parks and Wildlife estimates half a million pheasant and a million and a half quail bite the dust every year, and it's a safe bet all but ten of them will be served with raspberry Jell-O salad loaded with pineapple and whipped cream. Motels set out signs welcoming bird dogs and warning of a $100 fine for cleaning birds in your room.

Clem and the Boys at the Bar are still chewing on last year's hunt. They drove eighteen hours for a quarter-pound of meat, because you can't eat anything but the breast, but they got their limit before the dogs broke a point. The hunters had a lot to say about the state's ability to grow rest stops instead of trees for shade, build grain elevators bigger than the state capitol, and place historic markers overlooking feed lots. Shame about the sparrows, they agreed, having to nest in the "U" on the Jiffy Lube sign because there are no trees.

Something funny happens when the land gets flat. People still sit on the front porch, listen to the bug zapper, and spend Sunday afternoon poking the ashes in the burn barrel. They farm riverbeds, read books while driving, and refuse to shop without coupons. In Colorado we bet on the date of the first snow. In Kansas they wager on when water will come into the Arkansas River to win a shopping spree at the mall. Everyone in Kansas either has, or lusts for, a cabin in Colorado.

There has been a lot written about the plains, and Clem says it's all true. Soda is called "pop" and "damn" is a dirty word. Every little museum in every little town displays a Mason jar full of 1932 Depression dust. Conversations all start with "Hihowareya?" and end with "Haveaniceday!" even when it's 10 P.M. and the day is damn well over.

In the Heartland, kettlecorn is a delicacy. Green vegetables are not a food group and canned peaches are considered a vegetable.

White things are served on white plates, tone on tone, like creamed chicken on biscuits with white gravy. Not a flake of parsley to break the glare. In a country where you are invited to a "feed" or to "stuff your face," it is not surprising that Spam cupcakes beat out Sardine Cool Whip for a blue ribbon at the county fair. Applebee's is as gourmet as it gets.

The plains are filled with women who shouldn't wear shorts, kielbasa-faced dames who spend their lives looking at the Missouri River and thinking about where it might have taken them. They grow hostas with a vengeance and still use dishrags. Chicken-fried steak and mashers are on the diet plate, and the ladies from Weight Watchers ride on the Dairy Queen float in the Fourth of July Parade.

Men still play whist and hold doors open. Every one of them knows how to drive a grader and can give you directions to the landfill. They are addicted to ballgames, barbecue, and beer, not necessarily in that order, and they forsake NPR for farm reports on pork bellies and corn futures. They all want to hunt game in Colorado.

Kids eat TV dinners and end sentences with prepositions. Boys jam their fists deep into their jean pockets to make bulges where they wish they had them. Girls are born knowing how to make apple butter and custard pie. They grow up convinced that the "good life" means making enough money to buy a second car, a fridge with an ice-making machine on the door, and a vacation home in Colorado.

Clem and the boys did not linger in Kansas after the hunt. They didn't visit the Lesbian Dude Ranch in the Flinthills, the whirl-a-gig farm in Mullinville, or the barbed wire museum in Lacrosse. They passed up the bank in Norton that displays portraits of every losing candidate for president and exhibited little interest in the museum in a salt mine. They did not stop to participate in contests for cornhusking, pancake flipping, and lutefisk throwing. And they had no interest in the world's largest ball of twine, the world's largest prairie dog, or the world's largest outdoor concrete swimming pool. But they were sorely tempted to spit chew into the world's deepest hand-dug well.

No point in buying a newspaper. Who wants to read about school boards deciding to teach Creationism, a lady legislator arguing women should never have been given the vote, or the cost of replacing a 250-watt lightbulb on top of the capital with a statue of an Indian? The Boys at the Bar seriously considered staying home and watching the wheat grow on Kansas State University's website. Instead, they decided to toast Kansas by drinking the Marsala instead of pouring it over the pheasant, but you can be damn sure they'll be doing it while cleaning their birds in the sink at a Holiday Inn.

Thanksgiving Ain't for Turkeys

THE HOLIDAYS BRING OUT the worst in guys who wear steel-toed boots. Why can't they just pretend it's Saturday night, scrub down, and fake table manners for just one family dinner? Okay, so it doesn't begin and end with red beer at the Corral Club, and okay it *does* mean listening to Uncle Fred describe the one that got away, again. Of course Fred's too senile to remember whether he's describing an elk, a German Brown, or his first wife, but that's no reason to fall asleep in the mashers.

There is more than one way to entertain yourself at Thanksgiving dinner, and shooting peas at the kids should not be an option for adults. Crazydave-the-Plumber lies awake at night inventing options. One year he appeared at the table dressed in nothing but a loincloth, head shaved in a Mohawk, and held forth on Squanto's contribution to the history of North America. Crazydave was firmly convinced that the Pilgrims at Plymouth Colony would have starved to death if Squanto hadn't taught them how to fish and plant corn. In the World According to Crazydave, Squanto was the first American hero: guide, interpreter, and treaty-maker.

The Boys at the Bar regard Thanksgiving dinners as a challenge, not a meal. They are still talking about the year Merv, unbeknownst to his Old Lady, laced the stuffing with popcorn. Only way to know when the turkey's ready, he said. Listen for the popping sounds and when the turkey's done, it just blows out the oven door. Everyone remembers when Tex served porcupine, just like the town's first settlers, and when Aldus poured flaming cognac over the turkey, setting the dining room drapes on fire.

These kinds of antics are hard on the womenfolk who are quick to get mad and even. One year Agnes came out of the kitchen carrying a real live turkey, instead of the goose roasting in the oven, and presented it to her Old Man to carve. The turkey, just as nervous as Agnes, left droppings all over the kitchen while he gawked at the goose through the oven window. Erna shoved her Old Man's briefs into the cavity, surprising everyone when he ceremoniously spooned out the stuffing. Mary Jane claims the best Thanksgiving dinner she ever served was catered by the American Legion. Down at the Corral Club, where moderation is a cuss word, the boys still think turkeys are tourists, and elk roast is the only acceptable pièce de résistance for any holiday table.

Take Charlie's elk, for example—there was never anything quite as tasty. Charlie shot the big one out behind the dump. It was midnight and off-season, of course, but that wasn't the problem. The problem was, the elk took a flying leap into the sewer pond before he died. The way Ernie tells it, Charlie called at midnight, half crazy, so Ernie suits up for a hard night. He four-wheels out to the pond, pushes through the willows, lassoes a hind leg, drags five hundred pounds of carcass to shore, and dresses him out in full view of the gods of wastewater treatment. Ernie says it was the best elk he ever tasted and the Boys at the Bar are still debating why. Some think the meat was so tender because the water cooled it down so quickly, others swear it was the instant marinade. Walt says it was every bit as delicious as *his* elk, the one that died in a beehive and was instantly honey-cured.

Out at Dry Lake, this year's Thanksgiving dinner will be served at 4 P.M. when the family is so dang hungry they will eat anything. The recipe will come from L.L. Bean's *Wild Game Cookbook* and be roasted in a crockpot. There will be eggshells in the coffee and toothpicks for dessert. There will be three spices on the table: salt, pepper, and ketchup. You can bet there will be no ginger in the cranberries, no garlic in the mashed potatoes, and no oysters in the stuffing. Maybe just a touch of bourbon in the cook, especially if the game's on during dinner.

Cowboy Christmas

NOBODY HATES CHRISTMAS more than Crazydave-the-Plumber and his cronies, the Boys at the Bar. My Old Man celebrates the season by pointing out that he's receiving instead of giving, that he's made a list, checked it twice, and you're not on it. Some years he marches door-to-door delivering little bags of coal throughout the neighborhood.

His Christmas tradition is calling Santa at the local radio station to complain that the reindeer are poking holes in his roof and shaking the chimney bricks loose. He loves warning Santa that if he doesn't keep his ill-mannered reindeer off the roof, we'll be eating reindeer steaks for dinner. Our kids still think Santa eats pretzels and drinks Coors.

Crazydave is devoted to recycling Christmas cards. Every year he sends last year's cards, complete with family photographs and letters, to total strangers. Every card that comes in with a holiday wish is sent back out to someone who has never seen or heard of those people, their kids, or that dog. He claims he is doing people a favor by giving them something other than the economy to worry over. But the truth of the matter is, Crazydave would rather be down at the Corral Club than home reading *The Night Before Christmas*. He would rather drink beer than eggnog.

He is also sure Christmas trees wouldn't grow on secluded hillsides unless they were meant to be stolen. So he steals his tree, always after cocktails, always at midnight, and always from Tex's property out Twenty Mile Road. Tex is a buddy so he never says a word about the thefts, or Crazydave's spring trips into the woods to look for saws lost in snow banks. Tex does payback by stashing the tinsel-covered carcasses of his Christmas trees in Crazydave's chimney. Down on Laurel Street they celebrate the New Year by watching Ben's Crane Service extricate the tree from the chimney.

Tex wasn't much into holidays either. The Boys the Bar are still talking about the night he tired of watching the light on top of his Christmas tree blink, took down his .30-30, and shot it out. That might have been the year before he rode his pony, Chico, into the living room because it was so cold out in the stable. Or it might have been the year after he hung the ornament boxes on the tree because his Old Lady had asked him to "hang a box" every time he walked by. Tex took the assignment literally, and by day's end, the tree was covered with unopened boxes of tree decorations. Tex told some knee-slappers down at the Corral Club, but one Christmas Eve he dallied down there so long that his Old Lady had time to return his Christmas present and serve him divorce papers for dinner.

Another legendary Christmas dinner was ruined when Don took his pet goose, Mary Jane, to an elegant Christmas Eve dinner. The goose got nervous. It was hard to tell whether her angst was prompted by the amount of champagne she consumed or visions of becoming part of the spread, but Mary Jane transformed the lavish holiday table into a landing field and wiped out candelabra, crystal, silver, and china. Come to find out, she had a drinking problem and, ironically, she died from consuming too much Wild Turkey.

Crazydave was also fond of celebrating Christmas Eve at the Corral Club. He claimed he stayed down there to cheer up all the lonely guys who had nowhere else to go. I'm thinking, a couple more no-shows for the stocking hanging and *he'll* be the one with no place else to go. Then last year he came home early. He rushed into the kitchen and packed turkey, trimmings, and everything in the refrigerator into the pickup. He stole the tree and most every box under it and disappeared into the night.

Gone were the carefully wrapped flannel shirts I'd ordered for him from L.L. Bean. The new camping gear from Cabela's, the John Prine records, and the velveteen dress for our daughter, vanished. The box with seventeen bows from Aunt Agnes, which more often than not contained a glorious cashmere scarf, was missing. So were the homemade dog biscuits and unidentified package from Saks Fifth Avenue. I was madder than a mashed cat.

Come to find out, Crazydave took our whole Christmas over to Junkyard Rose's digs in the trailer park behind the dump. Junkyard Rose had red hair, bad teeth, and dozens of illegitimate children fathered by an equal number of drifters. That night we celebrated Christmas with Top Ramen noodles. It was the best holiday feast ever, but I suspect he never told the Boys at the Bar.

Getting Ready for the New Year

THANK GOODNESS the season to be jolly is over. Landfills are loaded with fruitcake, holiday suicide hotlines have shut down, the ball has dropped, and I've maxed out the scale and seventeen credit cards. It's time for the Stock Show, a sure sign that Colorado is heading into a new year.

The Chinese says it's the year 4702 and it doesn't begin until February 9. The Jews say it's the year 5765 and it begins October 3. I say it begins whenever I remember to change the date on letters and checks. This should be a very good year because I rigorously observed all the customs that assure luck.

I opened the door at midnight so the old year could escape, and smooched my honey so the future will be warm. I stocked the larder so there will be plenty to eat, and did the laundry so no one would wash away or die. I assured prosperity by paying all the bills, and stuffing money into everyone's wallets.

I hung mistletoe to keep ghosts away, draped a straw rope to invite happiness, set off firecrackers to scare away evil spirits, and hung lanterns to light the way for the New Year. I sprouted grains of wheat in a little dish, flew a kite, plunged with the polar bears, and let a carp free in a river.

I am exhausted.

I observed all the gustatory rituals. At the stroke of midnight I munched donuts like the Dutch, indulged in pickled herring like the Poles, and, like the Cubans, consumed twelve grapes, one for each month past. I dunked apples in honey and ate black-eyed peas, hog jowls, oyster stew, cabbage, rice, boiled cod, and buckwheat noodles.

I have indigestion.

Tradition holds that it is very good luck if the first person to enter the house on New Year's Day is a tall, good-looking stranger bearing a gift. I'm thinking, tall, good-looking strangers are welcome any day, but the first one to cross my threshold was the plumber with a Roto-rooter.

My pal Betsy starts the year by collecting pictures of all the things she aspires to in the year ahead. She glues them on a poster that she hangs in the kitchen. The year her display included a mink coat, a yacht, and a swimming pool, her husband asked for a divorce. Agnes freezes her credit cards in a block of ice until they are paid off, and Fred spends the first quarter recycling potpourri, bamboo steamers, and the singing jackalopes he receives for Christmas.

The Babylonians started the whole thing four thousand years ago by throwing an eleven-day party to welcome spring. They even had resolutions, the most popular of which was to return borrowed farm equipment. The Greeks introduced the baby as a sign of rebirth, but the baby was Dionysus, god of wine. We didn't get the calendar year until 46 B.C. when Julius Caesar decided to synchronize time with the sun and named January for Janus, the god with two heads, one looking forward, one looking back, a condition common to young mothers.

Truth is, everyone designs their own New Year. It can be ruled by stars, seasons, politics, or work. The athletic year begins with spring training and ends with bowl games. So January really is the end, unless you're a hockey player, in which case there is no beginning, or a basketball player, in which case there is no end. The birders' year sends veterans, hard-pressed to add new species to their Life Lists, searching for cheap air fares to remote parks and wildlife refuges to chase the elusive scarlet tanager and little green heron.

The dog year makes me feel young and the tax year make me feel poor, so until I canceled them, I let the birthday year rule my personal affairs and energy cycles.

No matter when it begins, I intend to make the world a better place in the year ahead. I will eat more chocolate, drink more champagne, and get a passport whether I need it or not. I will buy hardcover books, send my mother-in-law flowers on her birthday, and throw out the bridesmaid dress from my sister's wedding. I plan to clean the bookshelves to make room for new ideas, and to rearrange furniture, pictures, and plants so I have a new house without spending any money.

These are not resolutions, mind you, because like the U.N., I have trouble with resolutions. I have no plans to stick with the diet. I'm canceling my health club membership, and I know I'll forget to floss.

On Cuisine

Hunting Camp Gourmet

THERE IS SOMETHING about hunting season that makes testosterone levels peak. Men dress up like trees and spray themselves with elk urine. The father of your children looks into the mirror and sees an Indian. The game warden turns into an outfitter. Sales of white bread and peanut butter soar, and ibuprofen makes the Fortune 500 list. Everyone wants to turn Bambi into burgers.

One year I decided to find out why fifteen million people don scent-free camo and blaze orange to hike uphill both directions. I hired out as "Old Greasy," the camp cook for a full-service big game outfit in Colorado, home of the largest elk population in the world. Eat your heart out Pam Houston, I thought, I'm going to meet Tarzan and hear some record-mangling stories. I was wrong.

Despite getting up at 2:30 A.M. to have breakfast on the table at 4:00, we got along just fine. I make it clear right off that no one calls me "Honey," and they were just as straightforward about not being served foods with parsley or cracked pepper and, forgodsake, no spinach in the lasagna. Dinner is served at 9:00 P.M. and the pots are scrubbed by 11:00. In between I staggered bleary-eyed through the grocery store and thought about drinking the cooking sherry.

Valley View Outfitting, located in a downtown "castle" complete with sauna, is to big game hunting what Sun Valley is to skiing. They lease exclusive rights to thousands of acres of private land, and their guides leave no footprints. Their guests are baby boomers willing to pay $4,000 a week to come eyeball-to-eyeball with an elk without having to sleep on the ground.

Hunting camp transforms men who are bug marks on the windshield of life into extraordinary storytellers. Hunters have an uncanny ability to make a long story longer, but at hunting camp, they get to rehash with buddies who are too polite or too soused to interrupt or edit. That's why God created buddies and bartenders.

Hunting camp stories never have a punch line. Most revolve around I-saw-the-elk-and-the-elk-saw-me or youdda-hadda-been-there. Ever so often a profound truth will surface, like: Starting off lost is a helluva lot better than ending up lost. But, in most cases, plot lines are simple: the length of the noon nap, how far we walked today, who ate the most candy bars, whether or not you sat on your sandwich.

I'm tossing a salad when Sam begins to describe the make and model of his weapon. I'm peeling the potatoes while he relives an encounter. Two hours later, I'm pulling the meatloaf out of the oven and he's explaining why he missed the shot. By the time he sits down for dinner, I've finished the cooking sherry.

While the guides plot strategy—which ridge to stalk, whether to bugle like an aggressive bull or an amorous doe—Harry-the-Hunter explains how he filed for divorce the day his Lovely melted his fleece in the dryer. The hilarity is broken only when a homebound Honey calls to report she can't make the mortgage payment, has a brain-busting cold, and the transmission in the Jimmy is out. She points out he failed to execute his will before leaving, but what she really means is she's tired of his crazy mother, her nasty boss, and their truant kids. When will you be home? Isn't that when duck season begins?

Martha Stewart would hate hunting camp. The crepe pan is a forty-inch cast-iron skillet. No one likes paté de wapiti. The French toast is fried in bacon grease, and popcorn is the appetizer of choice. Pineapple upside-down cake is the only acceptable dessert. Bubba asks for "real" mustard, not the Grey Poupon or honey Dijon on the table, but the kind that comes in a yellow plastic bottle. Luke wants to know where he can find ice; it's in the freezer part of the fridge. I'm tempted to ask whether they keep it somewhere else in Sheboygan.

The real problem is sleep deprivation. By the time bow season ended and rifle season began, I had backed my car into a ditch, taken out a taillight, snapped at my best friend, and gained ten pounds. I was clearly a hazard, on the road and off. Although I invested my tip money in a chiropractor, masseuse, herbalist, and acupuncturist, nothing pumped adequate amounts of oxygen to my brain.

Next time I hear the Call of the Wild, take me to the edge of the woods and shoot me, split me open, and cool me down. Or just hand me the remote so I can turn on the Discovery Channel.

Cowboy Caviar

SPRING RITES OF PASSAGE commemorate graduation, confirmation, motherhood, weddings, and other new beginnings. In Colorado, it's a time of bawling, burning, and bloodletting. It's time to harvest the legendary Rocky Mountain oyster by relieving little lambs and calves of their manhood. Men wield hot irons and hot language and cattle are nervous.

Thousands of newborns are rounded up, branded, inoculated, and ear-tagged. Men squat in the dust ready to mark, Old Ladies cook for the crew, kids tally, and city-bred greenhorns tote the nut bucket. The Boys at the Bar claim farm oysters taste a lot like bald eagle or sandhill crane, but that may be just to tick off the guys down at the Division of Wildlife.

Rocky Mountain oysters, called "prairie oysters" east of the Divide and "fries" to the west, are also dubbed "barnyard jewels," "bollocks," "testy fries," and "Montana tenderloin." They are most frequently bull or calf nuts, although sheep, goat, buffalo, boar, turkey, and capon have also relinquished the right to be fathers, to the delight of patrons of bikers' bars, truck stops, and dance halls with mechanical bulls. They are served at places where credit cards are not accepted and no one drinks lite beer or drives under 100 miles an hour. They are always consumed with substantial quantities of banter, dirty dancing, wet T-shirt and cow chip throwing contests.

Today the testicle, once used to make soap in the fourteenth century, is achieving gustatory credibility. More than eight hundred websites provide incomplete guides to honky-tonks, events, a wide variety of recipes, and bad jokes about cutting them off, often with your teeth. Long the province of drunks, who love to boast about eating them raw, nuts are going gourmet. They have been discovered by the BMW and Jaguar crowd, which dips them in remoulade and chipotle sauce. Steakhouses serve them right along with Crab Louis, and the Jaycees and Explorer's Clubs throw Oyster Feeds for fundraisers. The intensity of interest among the culinary corps prompted the *Wall Street Journal* to investigate which wine best complements Swinging Sirloin. The winner was cabernet sauvignon, but out at the ranch, we're gonna stick with twist-offs.

At some ranches they just toss calf nuts on branding irons and eat them when they explode. But up at Dry Lake we've been serving filleted bull fries at a Nut Fry for three hundred of our most intimate friends for decades. A crew of renegades fries 'em in cast-iron skillets the size of Rhode Island, on a fire hot enough to splatter grease over a nine-mile radius. It takes two kegs to skin 'em out and four more to keep the cooks numb. The Secret Recipe for the batter has been secret for so long that no one can remember exactly whose secret it is. But it involves equal parts flour and mashed Rice Krispies, seasoned with paprika, garlic salt, and red pepper.

The Boys at the Bar, who scoff at people who don't have the cajones to eat nuts, have a lot to say about their preparation. Prompted by a few brewskis, they are transformed into gustatorial gurus, loaded with opinions on whether to marinate, scald, or soak; whether to dredge them in cracker or bread crumbs, corn meal or flour; whether to sauté, deep-fry, braise, or poach them; and whether to dunk them in chili or mustard, barbecue or horseradish sauce, ranch dressing or Cheese Whiz. Martha Stewart has taken no position, although her country cousin, Maisie Stewart, shares her favorite "tendergrown" recipes on a big ol' website.

In Colorado, Sam Arnold's Fort restaurant in Morrison promotes "critter fritters" to foreign dignitaries. Bruce's Bar in Severance has served enough "fries" to residents of Fort Collins, Greeley, and Windsor to enable its proprietor to drive a BMW. In fact, "oysters" have long been the pièce de résistance at emporiums in Denver and Dallas, and a cause for summer testicle festivals drawing thousands to Calgary, Missoula, Helena, Billings, Byron (IL), Vinta (OK), and Cass County (NE). The granddaddy of 'em all is in Clinton, Montana, where 15,000 people have been chowing down on 2.5 tons of battered bull nuts for twenty-something Septembers.

It may be worth the trip. After all, tiger testicles on rice are haute cuisine in the Far East. The *Kama Sutra* claims sweetened milk in which ram or goat testicles have been boiled increases sexual vigor. Giovanni Casanova loved them, as do gourmets in Spain, Italy, and France, where *animelles* are a pricey delicacy.

What's more, they're kosher.

Cowboy Appetizers

THE FIRST TIME my mother came West to visit, there was an elk in the bathtub. It had been poached, skinned out, and cured. It had grown a thin coat of light green penicillin by the time my mother, a connoisseur in matters of escargot and beef tartar, assumed command of a half dozen drunk cowboys.

She transformed an old door propped on sawhorses into a plein air butcher shop, and under her tutelage, a 400-pound wapiti was delicately transformed into rolled roasts, seasoned stews, and trimmed steaks, all wrapped and labeled for freezing. The Monforts could have taken a lesson.

As a rule, girls have to be careful when they take a cowboy back East to meet Mom. A lot of mothers have trouble with guys who spit chew, stash cigarette ashes in their jean cuffs, and keep their hats on in the house. My mother was the exception. She decided early on that Crazydave-the-Plumber was the perfect son-in-law. Of course, she was wrong.

No one could understand why the Queen of Eastern Effete would take to a guy who grew up in a Wyoming sheepwagon. It began at the wedding reception when her best friend Marybelle met the groom. "Well," says Marybelle to the cowboy, "what does the family think of you?"

"Frankly," says the cowboy to the dowager, "I don't give a rat's ass."

Well, someone told someone, who told someone, who told my mother, who decided this was the totally correct response.

From that moment on, her cowboy son-in-law could do no wrong. She would have none of it when I called to grouse about the way he ate crackers in bed, left toilets in the driveway, and failed to call when Happy Hour at the Corral Club proved more inviting than supper at home.

When we went East to visit, he walked her white poodle down Fifth Avenue. He fixed the dishwasher. She took him to the Bolshoi. He made her jerky. She promised never to tell anyone that he enjoyed Swan Lake.

I think she liked him because, like her husband, he had a total disregard for No Trespassing signs and traveled with a salt shaker in the car glove compartment so he was always prepared to stop to dine on tomatoes, cukes, and watermelon growing along backcountry roads. Both men were addicted to reading historic roadside markers and bringing home uncleaned fish. Neither ever pushed back from a table without declaring the meal the best he ever had.

My mother "did gourmet" long before Martha Stewart started making her own marshmallows. Her specialty was Chinese. She took courses on how to cook things in sauce—garlic, oyster, and sweet and sour. She haunted Chinatown markets and collected won ton soup bowls with ugly blue flowers. Egg rolls were her specialty.

The production of egg rolls requires a lot of time and cooking sherry. It takes endless hours of unskilled labor to mince, chop, and stuff the seafood and chicken, spices and veggies that keep the bamboo shoots company. Crazydave-the-Plumber and his pal Smokey-the-Carpenter were drinking Coors when, on a trip back East, my Mom recruited them to chop and stuff egg rolls destined for auction at a Democratic Party fund-raiser.

"Democrats cook," she said, "Republicans cater." When my mother wasn't in the kitchen, she consistently delivered three precincts to the Democrats. After a few rounds of Happy Days Are Here Again, she left the cowboys to handle stuffing and wrapping. Leaving drunk cowboys unattended in a kitchen, or anywhere else for that matter, is a social, economic, and political mistake. They immediately began to fill egg roll wrappers with dog food, which they froze to take back to the Boys at the Bar. This would be, they agreed, even more delectable than the Badger Balls they had barbecued for hors d'oeuvres on Valentine's Day.

But the boys forgot to take them home and, unfortunately, the ersatz egg rolls found their way to the auction table at the Democratic Party fundraiser, where they sold for massive amounts of money. My mother failed to see any humor in the caper. My father, long convinced that Herbert Hoover was America's greatest president, thought Alpo perfectly fitting for Democrats, and like the Boys at the Bar, said it was a real kick in the pants.

Coffee in a Tin Cup

IN THE '70S, guys rode into town on a Harley, described wild schemes, and scribbled numbers on a cocktail napkin while pulling on a longneck down at the Pioneer Bar. Maxine, the bank's gumsmacking, token lady loan officer, was absolutely not impressed. In the '90s, developers began jetting into town, packing $7,000 dirt bikes and holsters filled with Evian. Bank presidents were bedazzled. Today, the last ones over the Pass are still peddling bright new ideas, but the Boys at the Bar are pretty sure opening a Starbucks at the rodeo grounds isn't one of them.

The West is always being reinvented by change, much of it prompted by the invasion of railroads, mines, drought, and fast-buck artists. The latest challenge comes from overeducated, underemployed baby boomers who build second homes, wings on the arts center, and parks dedicated to their children.

The men have MBAs from fancy schools, and enough money to retire the national debt. Their ladies preside over trophy homes with plush living rooms and kitchens the size of football fields. They roam the High Country in Hummers, and their trust funds power the economy. They are replacing forests with ridge-top homes framed by forty-acre driveways, to the dismay of the Good Ol' Boys who struggled to grow grain in the '20s, vegetables in the '30s, coal in the '40s, ski areas in the '70s, and summer recreation in the '80s.

Blake is a product of the love-it-to-death '90s. He came into the county a few years back with a lot of education and buckets of Daddy's cash. He is one of a growing population of second-home owners who adore living in the Rockies as long as their roads are plowed and deer don't trample their gardens. To assuage his guilt at having been handed the family business, Blake wants to "give back to the community."

Blake has never tackled the challenges of dryland farming, beetle kill, water rights violations, fence-line trespass, or drought. He can afford the luxury of opening and closing main street businesses that fail to leap into the black. Blake says he wants to preserve the legacy of the valley. The Boys at the Bar say he's green-belting his trophy home, and as soon as the preservation easement is confirmed, the place will go on the market for millions more than the appraiser says it's worth.

Blake doesn't drink at the Corral Club.

Blake doesn't know a Holstein from a Hereford, but he's come up with a plan to rescue the rural economy. He buys his lettuce in prepackaged plastic bags, but he's got enough of the "real" green stuff to prompt a passel of bankers, some county extension types, a gaggle of do-gooders, a handful of ranchers, and a county commissioner or two to gather at the local grease trap to review his plan. Jefferson opened the West with a vision, now Blake wants to revitalize it by selling lattes at the rodeo grounds.

Blake and the ranchers meet over hamburgers, made from local beef of course, to examine his proposal to recharge the local economy with espresso. The idea was as popular as ice on a stock tank. All the beer in America, with or without shots, could not have sold the idea of introducing lattes, with or without caffeine, to the Boys at the Bar.

Someone suggested that the time might be better invested in addressing some of the more pressing threats to agriculture, such as federal land policies, grazing fees, reintroduction of the wolf, predator controls, and restrictive financing. Silence prompts Blake to observe that the problem with agriculture in our valley is that ranchers are too pessimistic. But, let's face it, only rich people can afford to be optimistic. Charles Darwin called it right: It's not the strongest or most intelligent who survive, it's the ones who are most responsive to change.

The Boys at the Bar have not been obsessing over the need for change or latte at the rodeo grounds. In fact, it has never come up. They think the world needs people who know how to grow wheat, pound it into flour, and bake bread. They are not looking to buy French wine and Florentine pottery from boutiques on Main Street. They do not lust after Gucci and Godiva, and they have little interest in Wednesday afternoon chamber music concerts. They want their coffee perked, not pressed—and they like drinking it out of a tin cup.

Sara Lee Is My Best Friend

SARA LEE IS my best friend. She makes reducing stress easy. Every time my life goes to Hell, I climb into bed with a Sara Lee Cherry Cheesecake and a fork. Not a slice, mind you, the entire 109 ounces, 15,890 calories and 287 fat grams, frozen solid. The trick is to eat the entire cake before (a) it defrosts, (b) you get caught, or (c) you are consumed by guilt.

Cheesecake is one of the four basic food groups. The other three are fettuccini Alfredo, chocolate, and pizza. I personally have never met a food I didn't like. I have always operated on the premise that if some is good, more is better. As a result, I have been overweight since the age of three when I could reach the refrigerator door, and despite a lifelong search, I still haven't found any non-food rewards worth a damn.

I don't care what Weight Watchers pays the Duchess of York to hype the salutary effects of non-food rewards: taking the Concorde to Paris, unlimited credit at Barnes & Noble, or opening a heart-shaped box containing a diamond tennis bracelet. These kinds of perks may serve as balm for the big stuff like when your mother dies, your husband has an affair with his secretary, your teenage daughter gets knocked up, or your son flunks out of the community college, but when the paste is all squeezed out of the toothpaste tube of life, the only solace is food. Peggy turns to banana splits. Susan does margaritas. Barbara thinks Peking duck at the Jade Palace is better than a week at the Golden Door, and Joanne is convinced that chocolate is an essential part of the Trinity.

Let's face it, girls, the only way to turn a downer into an upper is food, preferably loaded with calories. The only way to cope with the physical and psychological ramifications of life's everyday trauma is food, preferably laced with chocolate. The only way to balance home, office, and inner self is food, preferably packed with sugar. A leaf of lettuce drizzled with low-fat dressing just doesn't cut it.

Madison Avenue said I could have it all: live in the burbs, drive a minivan, and raise 2.4 above-average children. You can get the kids to soccer, the dog to the vet, overdue books back to the library, and the car in for a lube. But it's all easier with cheesecake. I've been eating Sara Lee cheesecake since I failed Latin at the National Cathedral School for Girls. I really didn't care about the structure of sentences or cities, and I knew I was never going to join a bridge club.

I know people who swear by the healing powers of Prozac, Saint-John's-Wort, and 12-step programs, but my salvation has always been cheesecake. It helped me cope with college in my '20s, career crisis in my '30s, a full nest in my '40s, and an empty nest in my '50s. It has been my salvation in widowhood, retirement, caring for elderly parents, and burying best friends. Now I'm forced to confront my mortality. I must execute a living will, pick an executor, label the family pictures, and clean the garage. It's time to examine tax shelters, nursing homes, health insurance, and Rand McNally's seventeen best places to spend your dotage. You cannot do these things without cheesecake.

I've tried the cold shower, with and without a loofah, and the hot bath, with and without Epsom salts. I know the value of retreating into a good book and walking the dog. I align my body at a chiropractor, my head at yoga, and my house with feng shui. I graze on ginseng for energy, ginkgo bilboa for memory, black cohosh for hot flashes, goldenseal for hemorrhoids, valerian for insomnia, angelica for nerves, burdock for hair loss, and feverfew for sweats.

But nothing works like cheesecake. I keep a half dozen in the freezer for emergencies. In fact, they are so essential to survival that I pay full price, no waiting for a sale, no double coupons. No last-minute rushing to the store because you never know when the need for a cheesecake fix will surface: overdrawn at the bank, empty mailbox on Valentine's Day, the gas bill triples, four points for going the wrong way down a one-way street, an audit notice from the IRS.

A day that demands cheesecake begins with no hot shower because the hot water heater konked out and ends with concocting nachos for the Old Man's poker club. In between the dog eats my $95 shoes, the car runs out of gas downtown, I get four points for speeding to the soccer game, and I throw my back out on the sixteenth load of wash. Sara Lee cheesecake is the only way to cope with days like this.

A pox on leafy green vegetables, V-8 juice, and fresh fruit. I'm available to testify that Jean Harris would not have killed Dr. Scarsdale if he would have let her eat just a tiny bit of cheesecake.

On Pals

Girlfriends

GIRLFRIENDS ARE HARD to come by and way more fun than therapy. They are playmates, cheerleaders, gossips, confidants, and shrinks. They know how to remedy problems, whether of our own making or not, and they share secrets, earthshaking or not. They know when to show up and whether to bring wine or chocolate, casseroles or artichoke dip.

Girlfriends laugh at us and with us. They know who they are and who you are. They help us give birth, get married, and raise children. They are there when you change husbands, jobs, and attitudes. They know our unspoken thoughts and can finish our sentences. They help us survive the loss of friends and the death of parents. They help us weed our yards and our lives. They tell it like it is, not like we may want to hear it, frequently over coffee and sometimes over a martini.

Girlfriends were created to promote indulgence, especially on facials, new bras, and hardback books. They are the guard dogs who will tell us when it's time to bag the peek-a-boo thong, color the hair, and think about a gluten-free diet. Who else will advise your Old Man that you want a black satin nightie for Christmas or convince you not to divorce him when he buys a John Deere to mow the yard instead?

Husbands, mothers, sisters, and children come with baggage, but girlfriends don't care whether you pay the mortgage, inherit the family silver, or donate to the Audubon Society. They invite your ex over for dinner when he comes to town. They visit your ninety-year-old mother at the nursing home. They babysit the kids while you get a root canal, and the dog when you have an out of town tryst. They will make spinach squares for you to take to the book club and brownies when you need something for the Girl Scout meeting.

Girlfriends are your alter ego. They may not tell you when you are right but they will always tell you when you're wrong—they will give advice whether you ask for it or not. They know when to ignore the ironing and the machinations of your teenage daughter, and when it's time to stop breastfeeding and to start losing weight. They will be there when your son flunks out of college and your daughter gets knocked up. They serve a major function: to tell you that you're not crazy.

While guys are lollygagging on the couch, girlfriends always have *big plans* to bike, hike, and misbehave. Girlfriends go on "field trips" to museums, concerts, and funky little B&Bs. They know when you, and therefore they, need to get away from the spouse, kids, and bridge club. So they make the reservations, pack the "travelers," and with next to no notice, swing by for lunch, an afternoon at a gallery, a day at the spa, or a weekend in the mountains.

They loan you books, give you gift certificates for massages, and make casseroles when company shows up unannounced. Mostly, they listen to endless stories about our nosey neighbors, whacked-out mothers-in-law, and SOB bosses. They stand ready to remind us that no one promised you a rose garden, and that sometimes it's okay to nip at the cooking sherry. Girlfriends can finish our sentences because they know us better than we know ourselves. They know whether we need downtime or cheesecake, and they're always ready to prowl the next yard sale.

My friend Susan grows flowers and children. She travels with her pockets loaded with Band-Aids for the kids and quarters for the carwash. Once she presented me with a pottery bowl she bought at an auction for some do-good organization because it reminded her of me. Small wonder, I had donated it to the sale.

My pal Peggy is a gustatory guru. Our friendship began when I sent my husband over to her house to borrow Kitchen Bouquet for the Thanksgiving gravy and she sent him home with a bunch of flowers. Forty years later I still call her every Thanksgiving morning to ask how to make gravy.

My playmate Jane invented naughty. She dances on barroom table tops, writes letters to the editor, and torments telephone solicitors with gusto. We have been exploring unmarked roads for longer than most marriages last.

My girlfriends put the Sisterhood of the Traveling Pants, the Ya-Ya's, and the Sweet Potato Queens to shame. Makes me think how much better off men would be if they had real girlfriends.

Chuck-the-Hero

SIX OLD BOYS from the legendary Tenth Mountain Division's Company L buried one of their own in a hillside cemetery overlooking Steamboat Springs last week. Staff Sergeant Chuck Hogue lived and loved, and was loved there, and it was time to say goodbye. We looked at the Purple Heart, bronze battle stars, and Good Conduct Medal he earned in combat at Kiska and Mt. Belvedere, and we filled the Bear River with tears.

Chuck came into town to ski and party with his buddies from Camp Hale during the war. When it was over he returned to marry the homecoming queen, raise five kids, and use his big hands to squeeze a living from the land. He dedicated his life to making things grow: cattle and family, hay and children, grain and values. And Chuck harvested Colorado's finest crops: good kids, good friends, good stories, and good times.

No one knows just how many roast lambs he slathered with garlic and lemon juice, or how many bonfires he shared with friends, from Pennsylvania where he grew up, from Camp Hale where he trained, from Lake Havasu where he golfed, and with an extensive community he fathered on the Hogue Ranch on the banks of the Yampa River. He taught us to sing and cuss with the best of them.

Chuck said he lived by three principles: keep your head down, always have a knife on the swather, and booze is the only answer. His life was filled with hound dogs, funky old hats that looked like they had been sat on precisely because they had been, and lame ditties he loved to recite around the campfire.

He fought for liberty and he bought American. He drank Dickel and Gatorade and ate his steak medium rare until his teeth gave out. He loved the sound of big bands, the songs of Willie Nelson, and the humor of Baxter Black. He played poker, drove Pontiacs, and read *Engineering News Record*. He survived the Depression, sixteen presidents, five wars, war injuries, and heart surgeries.

Chuck was humble, honest, and generous. Like most ranchers, he was a man of faith. Faith equipped him to fight weather, whitetop weeds, and insects. Faith enabled him to cope with interest rates, market prices, and government controls. He said a prayer before breakfast and at the family dinner table every night. In between he helped launch the co-op, the woolgrowers association, and three bowling leagues.

This big, roughhewn man found pretty, petite Babe Squire at a dance at the Mesa Schoolhouse. After only two dates, he showered her with poems and letters for three years, while he was away at war. And when he came back they joined hands, fifty-eight years ago. Together they fought anything that threatened the harvest and they danced up a storm on Saturday nights. They raised kids who knew how to juice cows, pull calves, shoot ducks, trap beaver, and cut sagebrush out of fence lines.

Chuck fished King Solomon Creek and hunted the forest above Big Creek. He went fishing with nothing more than a skillet, butter, and worms from the irrigation ditch. He hunted with a .30-40 Krag with open sights. The boys say he always walked the farthest and came back with the most. They remember him screaming at them for forgetting to clean the chaff out of the back of the combine or failing to milk the cows when they were supposed to. "The older you get, the dumber you get," he'd bellow. But it was always bark and never bite. The threatened boot in the seat of the pants was seldom delivered.

Fact is, Chuck's School of Broken Knuckles created a work ethic that continues to serve his ranch, the valley, and the future well. Chuck met the poet's definition of success: "He lived well, laughed often, and loved much. He enjoyed the trust of a pure woman, the respect of intelligent men, and the love of little children. He left the world better than he found it."

But his days on the swather are over. It was fitting that the town said its goodbyes in the church he plastered with his own hands. Chuck always said he wanted to live as long as John Doe and one day more. That day just passed. The time has come for his departure and as the Apostle Paul urged, he fought the good fight, finished the race, and kept the faith.

Now, it's Tee Time in Heaven.

Crazydave-the-Plumber

THE WORLD NEEDS plumbers more than it needs poets. Any plumber will tell you so. Plumbers are totally convinced that plumbing sustains the health of the nation. The history of democracy and the universe can only be explained by the availability and use of water. Use it or lose it—and shoot the guy who abuses it. Their creed is simple:

Righty tighty, lefty Lucy.
Shit runs downhill.
Don't bite your fingernails, and
Payday's on Friday.

Regardless of whether they are thin or paunchy, rack guns or fishing poles, plumbers are thick as thieves. They share parts and gossip. Most any time you can find them parked out on Twenty Mile Road, leaning on the tailgates of their trucks, fixing prices. They have Little Black Books that record the location of every grease trap and shut-off valve installed since Thomas Crapper wore knickers.

They live by a strict code: Reduce prices for little old ladies living on Social Security; quadruple rates for clients who help; never show the whites of your eyes to anyone who questions a bill; constantly remind the world that it is essential not to flush feminine hygiene products (affectionately known as "white mice").

Plumbers leave whisky bottles under houses, forget pliers under sinks, and hide "dead soldiers" (used water heaters) in city Dumpsters. If you ask for a refund for an unused forty-five-cent wye, every plumber in the county will know by morning and your service calls will go unanswered for life. Call 911 if you ever find one who has all the parts for your job on the truck, one who can complete a project without seventeen trips to True Value while the water is turned off.

Don't mess with the plumber because they know things you might want to know. They saw the raccoon run into the water line at the Ramada, but because the builder was a know-it-all, they decided not to mention the corpse in the filter. Everyone at the Corral Club knew, and to this day, none of their Old Ladies frequent the Ramada. They knew the city shouldn't have paved Oak Street before the water lines were replaced, but because the city council members were know-it-alls, there was no need to mention the leaks.

Plumbers don't have to be radio-dispatched because they have CBs, the real umbilical cord to what is, isn't, or may be happening. Without it you might not know how the plumbing inspector reacted when he found a rubber snake wrapped around the service line in the darkest corner of the crawl space at 7th and Laurel. The building inspector doesn't find that kind of stunt funny. The Boys at the Bar, on the other hand, see it as a clear call for another round.

Any plumber will tell you that the Eleventh Commandment demands that the plumber be paid. Plumbers have "doctor's bags" for clients who don't pay. A "doctor's bag" contains paper towels to plug pipes, nerf balls to stop up toilets, and marbles to clog drains. Trust me, it's cheaper to pay the plumber than it is to hire a backhoe to remove a softball wrapped in tape from a vent pipe. Plumbers can really be quite unreasonable about their bills.

When a guy down the street decided not to pay for a new hot water heater, Crazydave pulled the switch on his electric box in the middle of a ten-degrees-below-freezing night. The house froze, pipes burst, and the living room turned into an ice-skating rink. An ice cream parlor that failed to honor a sewer cleaning bill found giant cockroaches dancing in the cookies 'n' cream. An antique popcorn wagon, transformed into a sandwich shoppe, was lassoed and hauled over a cliff. An unpaid sewer cleaning bill at a la-de-da restaurant covered the cost of the company Christmas party.

No one can remember which of these capers landed Crazydave in the slammer.

He spent his jail time correcting plumbing sorrows about which the American Civil Liberties Union had been complaining to the county commissioners for years. He parked his big red plumbing truck behind the courthouse and rerouted pipes with the help of an embezzler and a rapist. The Boys at the Bar agreed he looked swell in an orange jumpsuit, and lined the alley to watch him jog two blocks to the hardware store for parts.

The county commissioners had no problem paying for parts, but as the board chairman pointed out, "time" was precisely what he was doing in jail so there was no-way-in-hell it could it be considered billable. Crazydave was still in the slammer when the cops and the bank, which held the mortgage on the popcorn wagon, figured out that it headquartered the biggest drug ring in town. It was a big time for the Boys at the Bar because they seldom got to celebrate the sheriff *and* the bank president getting stiffed on the same day.

Glen-the-Fisherman

IT'S SPRINGTIME in the Rockies and the Boys at the Bar are relishing the true joys of fishing: thinking about it before you go and lying about it after you get back. The age-old debate between stream and lake fishermen continues down at the Corral Club. But no one is arguing about the fact that fishing in chummed waters with a night light is the most fun you can have outside the law. Fish caught in violation of park service restrictions simply taste better.

My pal Glen has pulled more fish out of Pearl Lake than any bear, beaver, or man, and the Division of Wildlife knows it. Licenses, legal limits, no trespassing signs, and flies-and-lures-only regulations have never impaired his ability to catch-and-consume. Why anyone would pull a fish out of water and not eat it is beyond his comprehension. Years ago, before he traded Coors for café latté, Glen was number one on the Division of Wildlife's Most Wanted List. The boys in green would hide in the willows waiting for him to launch his antique rowboat with the fifty-year-old, nine-horsepower engine and eight-hundred-pound tackle box.

Glen fishes lakes, but never without a cooler full of dry ice hidden on the bank. He takes his brother Fillmore along, not so much for the company as for his willingness to run the cooler back to town on the way to church on Sunday morning. The fish rangers are fully aware that the freezer on Glen's back porch contains the very finest pink-fleshed trout, and Glen knows damn well that fish in the freezer legally qualify as "in possession." But they seem to have developed a "don't ask, don't tell" relationship.

Glen's buddy Crazydave fishes streams. He has spent the better part of his pre-Medicare years crawling through willows on his belly because, as he so frequently pontificates, if you can see them, they can see you. Crazydave is a threat to the brookie population of northwest Colorado. No one can challenge his record, fifty-seven ten-inch cutthroats in one afternoon, and no one ever caught him with night crawlers on a hook because he would cut the line with the light on the end of the Marlboro always hanging from his mouth.

These guys are the reason browns and rainbows are endangered in vast areas of the High Country and scores of game and fish officers have opted for early retirement. Glen figures fish have cost him a penny a pound, what with the cost of blackberry brandy, KFC carry-out, and $500 a year for dry ice. In lean years the boys cut up fish for bait. Glen swore by guts; Crazydave by eyeballs. Between them they buried enough fish guts on the lake's west bank to grow corn thirty feet tall. It's a wonder the smell never caused a bear attack.

The high cost of garden hackles prompted Glen and Crazydave to start their own nightcrawler farm. They turned a claw-footed bathtub in the backyard into a worm ranch and rounded up the big ones that come out to mate on the courthouse lawn after a drenching rain. But, oddly enough, there were never any worms in the bathtub when it was time to round 'em up for a fishing trip. Surprise midnight shoveling raids failed to locate the worms as did attempts to shock them out of the ground with a car battery tester. It didn't take too much Budweiser for the Boys at the Bar to conclude that the worms escaped because the worm ranch wasn't fenced.

Glen drives a Chevy and Crazydave drives a Ford, and the only thing they agree upon is that fish should be cooked on a stick and eaten head-to-tail, backbone and all. There it ends. Crazydave says the only reason to fish a lake is because streams are muddy in the spring. Like the guys at the new frou-frou Baite Shoppe, he says you're more apt to find a rocket scientist fishing a stream than a lake. Glen is equally dismayed by fly fishermen. He says it's a clear-as-day fact that catch-and-release guys would land more fish if they kept their hook in the water. And, if it's such a problem, he'd be more than happy to have them catch-and-release right into his creel.

Carla-the-Soccer-Mom

My friend Carla is the only person I know who sifts flour when a recipe calls for it. She does it once, twice, three times, depending on the instructions. I would not dream of sifting presifted flour, or any other kind for that matter.

I say Monica Lewinsky doesn't sift the flour. Carla says she isn't a Mighty Mite Soccer Team Mom. Carla says she will be the only mom who shows up with pound cake from Stonehenge. Her son will be humiliated. She'll never bond with the other mothers. She's too old for this kind of pressure.

In fact, Carla is an "older" mother. She's fifty-one and her son just turned twelve, but Carla's problem is not age related. She can keep up with the playground crowd. She biked the thirty-mile marathon, uphill both ways. She's a member of two book clubs and juggles a high-tech job with high-step aerobic classes. She still looks good in a bikini and has her PMS under control. It would be easy to hate her.

Until she was asked to bring something to the bake sale, Carla had no problem with motherhood. She was always available to pick up 67 gallons of Gatorade or to chauffeur the team to a game 407 miles east of Nowhere. Now they wanted her to bake. They had pushed the stress button and the problem was quite simple. Carla doesn't know how to bake.

Carla is firm in the conviction that supermarkets in America stock enough baked goods to accommodate all the birthdays, anniversaries, and potluck dinners in her life, and for that matter, the life of the nation. She maintains Madeleine Albright would sift three times just like the recipe. "You're not Madeleine Albright," I countered. You would have thought I had suggested an impeachable offense, and sifting had deep psychological ramifications.

I had never really thought too much about sifting: what it says about your relationship with your mother; how it will impact your son's performance in college; whether it reflects upon your marital relationship; is it a product of your socioeconomic status; does it make a statement about your political or sexual preferences?

When the snow gets deep in northwest Colorado and the only demands upon our time are to mend harness and throw hay to cows, we have time to ponder things, like whether or not to sift presifted flour. Three-wire winters provide time to peruse cookbooks received as wedding presents from a long-forgotten first marriage. They afford the leisure that gourmandettes like me need to ponder the many uses of baking soda; to think about some of the cookbooks that I should write, like *Escargot at Hunting Camp, How to Microwave the Cat*, and *What the Hell Is Kugel?*

Although the *Cake Bible* claims sifting is best accomplished by stirring with a fork, authoritative websites recommend using a mixer. I rushed to the library to see whether Martha Stewart had taken a stand. Silly me, she grinds her own flour. So I turned to the highest source, the Cookbook Queens in the Yampa Valley Cocktail Society. No-way-in-hell, they agreed, when polled during a focus group on whether tummy control panels in swimsuits really work.

But Carla persisted. She sifted three times. The cake soared to soufflé heights and then crashed. Cooled, it bore a remarkable resemblance to a cowpie. It's the altitude, she said. In the Rockies we blame everything, including the sex of the eldest child, on the altitude. Altitude explains the weather, burnt toast, and teenage acne. It does not, however, justify sifting flour just because the recipe calls for it.

Aristotle probably explained it best when he observed that men might not ask for directions, but women have never been known to follow them.

Laurie-the-Hairdresser

MY HAIRDRESSER is certifiably nuts. She's blonde by impulse and has lots of pierced body parts. She wields a razor and opinions with equal dexterity, and she is convinced that ferrets will inherit the earth.

It is hard to relate to the intensity with which my hairdresser can discuss ferret patterns, points, and tail length. She is up on lawsuits pitting health departments in California and New York, which want to ban ferrets as pets, against ferret-lovers and humane societies. She is deeply concerned about the color, temperament, conformation, and chromosomes of kit, not kin.

Suggesting that her darling Cinnamon Puff may be a rat's cousin will ruin both her day and your "do." She is a child of the '90s, and children of the '90s have exotic pets—like the guy down the street who beds a boa constrictor in his dresser drawer and walks him on a leash.

Personally, I've never wanted to snuggle with a weasel. My pet of choice since I was twelve remains the yellow Labrador. Yellow Labs regard ferrets as lunch meat, but my friend Helen deeply loved hers. He came from Pets R Us and had free run of the house until he ate her parka and required a $300 surgery to remove zipper fragments from his gut. Helen went on Prozac the day he died on the operating table.

You wouldn't think such a small furry animal would require so many support systems to promote, protect, and sustain it. But ferret owners are organized into leagues, associations, and clubs. They are networked by websites, chat rooms, and newsletters. They boast a photograph gallery devoted exclusively to ferrets, and a magazine featuring a ferret pinup centerfold. Calendars, cards, clip art, posters, and jewelry immortalize every twitch of the whisker. Shows, symposiums, and expos analyze their every idiosyncrasy. The world is littered with rescue and rehab centers, shelters and bite information banks, all devoted to this little mammal.

Everyone knows, wailed my friend Cindy, that ferrets are related to weasels and mink, and not to mice and hamsters. Cindy's ferret lived wild and free in the kitchen, eating table scraps, sleeping in a little cage overlooking a backyard full of apple trees. He was, unfortunately and unbeknownst to Cindy, lounging in the dishwasher when she pushed the start button. Cindy's now on Prozac too.

I'm not sure whether my hairdresser was on Prozac before or after ferrets came into her life. She broke a long-awaited appointment for a trim when Cinnamon Puff came down with influenza this winter. I guess he didn't get a flu shot because he died in February, and because the backyard was frozen solid, he was loaded in a Ziploc bag and stashed in the freezer to await proper interment in spring.

But every time the freezer opens, his body bag crashes to the floor. This upsets my hairdresser, who devotes a great deal of time to examining her true inner feelings about ferrets with both her $90-an-hour shrink and her $90-an-hour perm customers. I'm thinking this is the true balance in nature. I pay the hairdresser, she pays the shrink.

Nancy-the-Collector

THERE IS NOTHING as final as throwing away a guy's eyeglasses. It means he's dead—never coming back. Never again going to take out the trash, mow the yard, or kiss you goodnight. He's never again going to leave the toilet seat up, throw underwear on the floor, mangle the toothpaste, mix the whites and the darks in the wash. He's history and you don't have to worry about him taking up too much of the bed, falling asleep with the television on, or forgetting to call when he's going to be late for dinner. No tab at the Cork and Bottle. No shirts to iron. No ring 'round the tub. No shit in the driveway. There's nothing left to clean or bitch about.

This presents a problem for my cousin Nancy, who is constitutionally incapable of throwing anything away. Her idea of spring-cleaning is mailing off a picture or two from piles splattered across every dresser top in the house. Nancy has never served a meal on her dining room table because she's convinced it serves a higher purpose as the family archive. Last Christmas I sent her a box of heavy-duty trash bags. But taking out the trash was never one of Nancy's chores as a child, so there is no reason to believe that scattering family remains is going to be a function of her maturity.

What's more, Nancy firmly believes in family togetherness, even if the family is in ashes. Mom is in an urn in the kitchen. Dad is on the mantel in the living room. Tom the Cat is boxed in the foyer, finally safe from Bismarck the Dog, who is stashed in his bowl in the garage. Nancy's house is tidy but you definitely want to inquire before opening any containers with lids.

So when Nancy's husband of thirty years died last month, I began to fret. Not because she couldn't handle various stages of grief, cooking for one, or life without sex. She simply didn't have any more shelf space. There was no tradition of packing up the past and moving on. Her husband Ernie was clearly destined for a vase on the nightstand. This afforded Nancy the control she did not enjoy when he was alive because Ernie was something of a rounder.

The Boys at the Bar called him the Silver Fox because he effortlessly attracted broads and booze. He always exceeded his quotas, whether selling cars, plumbing parts, or aluminum siding; whether women, horses, or dogs; whether elk, deer, or quail. He loved the West because it accommodated his appetites, which, like his laugh, were hearty. Ernie ate ribeye and mashers, and peas off a knife. All he ever wanted from life was the wind at his back. Ernie used jars to store nails, moonshine, and pencil stubs. He wasn't the kind of guy who deserved to be stuffed into one. But God has a sense of humor about where we bury our dead.

Ernie's buddy Crazydave died from carbon monoxide poisoning while cleaning the garage. He loved his garage. We buried his ashes under a cottonwood tree on the banks of the Green River, midway between his two favorite fishing spots: The upstream hole in the shadow of a limestone ledge, and the downstream hole at the bend beyond the willows. The sacred fishing grounds were hidden in Utah's piñon-covered red dirt country, just beyond the cut made by the pipeline. They were sacred because they were remote enough to permit Crazydave to fish without a license and use worms in a lures-only area. It was fitting that by the time we carried his ashes down to the shade of the cottonwood tree, the area had been posted, "No Trespassing."

Ernie's pal Nell died of a heart attack while cleaning her basement. Actually, she had spent an enormous part of her life down in the basement, doing laundry and rearranging all the stuff her kids refused to haul to their own homes. We bawled something terrible when we stuck a longneck Bud in the red cowboy boot perched on her casket. Her kids, all of whom left home days before, or days after, they graduated from high school, finally emptied the basement. They also invested big bucks in an expensive memorial, an elegant engraved marble bench in the town cemetery. The Boys at the Bar were not at all surprised that by the time they visited the memorial, pigeons had pooped all over the shiny slab.

So get with it, Nancy. Clean the garage, empty the basement, and tidy up the yard. The shed has been a mess for forty years. Nothing you can do will eliminate the clutter of Ernie's life, but I would sure appreciate not bumping into him when I'm looking for the sugar.

Maude-the-Widow-Woman

MAUDE IS LOOKING for a replacement husband. Old Henry, tired of running the hardware store, just up and died several years ago. This left Maude with no one to change the oil in the Chevy. Of course Old Henry was literally and figuratively along in years but he had enough State Farm to permit Maude to get a perm and a pedicure. She was starting to feel kinda sassy when the pump went out. That's when Maude decided she needed a deputy spouse, a handy husband, someone who could jury-rig the pump.

Maude says Toni Morrison is right, nobody wants a sixty-year-old woman, except maybe grandkids and dogs. So when two respectable ladies in the bridge club found significant others in the personals columns, Maude marched right down to the drugstore newsstand. Searching the personals in a gazillion different kinds of magazines was harder than she thought. She scrutinized every bold, underlined, and italicized word for hidden meaning. She spent hours analyzing grammar, content, and style.

By the time the pharmacist was threatening to charge rent, she had concluded that person-to-person advertisers are all looking for slender, blonde, good-looking, self-assured, honest, outgoing, romantic, well-read, warm-hearted, successful, intelligent, ambitious, compatible, attractive, educated, sincere, responsible, spunky, smart, loving, playful, romantic, adventurous, independent, athletic, sensitive, unencumbered, multi-lingual ballroom dancers. On a good day I can juggle one or two of these acts, she thought.

"Men Seeking Women" all promise adventure, fun, and long-term relationships. They are all warm-hearted and ready for luv and, without exception, are meaningful soul mates, conscientious companions, and passionate lovers. They long to share rainbow days and star-studded nights. It made her tired. They want nymphets with whom to watch the sun set and the moon rise. Maude never got out of bed before noon. They lust after women who do aerobics, but Maude was Cleopatra in a former life. They want gals who tend to their gardens and cholesterol with equal fervor. She found it quite depressing.

The number of magazines carrying personal columns was equally discouraging. It became pretty clear pretty fast that guys named Tex don't advertise for companions in the *Tofu Times*, and no one named Montgomery wants to meet someone who reads *Agriculture Anonymous*. After a long and arduous search, Maude called the other day to share the following "Men-Seeking-Women" ads she found in a variety of magazines.

Blue Hair Gazette: Slender, blonde, financially secure veteran of 12-step programs, book clubs, and cook clubs; w/o chiropractic, dental, or surgical needs; partner and friend w/o family commitments; competency in tennis, golf, bridge; real estate in Palm Springs, Aspen, and St. Kitts a plus; poolside experience essential.

Treehugger Times: Slender, blonde vegetarian nonsmoker w/clean body and soul born in rainforest, desert, or swamp; comfortable above/below sea level, salt/fresh water, sweltering/frigid climes; into organic food, gardening, alternative medicine; mountain bike and North Face gear essential; prefer catch/release fisherperson with current Sierra Club or Audubon Society membership.

Redneck Review: Slender, blonde, home-schooled zealot willing to share prejudices about race, creed, color, sexual preferences, and handguns; closed mind and banged-up Bible essential; must be pro-life, apple pie, school vouchers, and the flag; former Tupperware/Avon sales experience a plus; willing to maintain a little white church in the Wildwood.

Entrepreneur Enterprise: Slender, blonde Cindy-Crawford look-alike; prefer Smith College graduate and/or Fortune 500 CEO; top physical/intellectual/financial shape; must look good in Benetton shorts, Bogner togs, Harley leathers; Pepsodent smile; into crème brûlée, horses, meaningful conversation, and life in the fast lane.

Celestial Sentinel: Slender, blonde, crazy, sexy, cool, far out, awesome, astrologically fit extraterrestrial; cosmic outlook; tuned in to essential oils, holistic medicine, and punk/rock/folk/reggae; limited material needs/desires; prefer vegetarian with current membership in Alternative Health Food Cooperative.

Western Ways: Slender, blonde roommate on cattle, horse, hay ranch needed to feed, clean, handle stock; mend fence and walk ditches; operate/repair machinery/heavy equipment; cook/keep house for hired men and dudes; tolerance for sage, chew, and cheap bourbon; border collie, blue heeler or dingo a plus; Ford pickup and Bronco season tickets essential.

Millie-the-Life-Coach

ONCE UPON A TIME we were a nation of ranchers and miners, lumberjacks and builders. We rose when the rooster crowed at the break of day, ate a hearty breakfast, toiled in the hot sun and freezing rain, got paychecks on Friday, and took baths on Saturday night. But times have changed. Today we are life coaches, image makers, and marketing consultants. We take courses in leadership, feng shui, and management. We hire consultants to mold our bodies, wardrobes, and lifestyles.

We are enchanted with process and procedure—strategizing has become a national pastime. We do it for money and men, adventure and love, and prime-time TV. In the '70s we closed the smelters and the mills and began teaching tactics instead of skills. We have built a nation of planners. Now we hire consultants to plan our weddings, careers, estates, and vacations. We spend megabucks developing sustainable communities, land use, marketing, and technology. We build massive federal, state, and local agencies to design policy and procedure for education, housing, health, families, and emergencies. We babble about goals and empowerment. We spend massive amounts of time listening to inspirational speakers, reading self-help books, and contemplating our navels.

Frankly, strategizing gives me hemorrhoids. I hate looking at someone's backside while they scratch key phrases on a big white pad with a Magic Marker—gives me the willies. I'm tired of Power Point presentations, listening to someone read bulleted items off a screen so big I can see it without my bifocals—makes me feel stupid. I can get all the information I need down at the water cooler, unlike my boss who is addicted to memos and meetings.

Every Thursday morning my boss Millie gathers the staff around a big round table littered with crayons, Silly Putty, Slinkies, scissors, and stickers to inspire creativity. The conference room is turned into a Scrapbook Barn and everyone doodles and blathers about contextualizing ideas, developing paradigms, and finding parameters. Sometimes we wash it all down with coffee and Danish because it's always easier to talk loaded with caffeine and sugar. Mostly we do more calories than content.

Millie is the queen of actualization and communication. She spends more time at leadership conferences than she does in the office. She's never at her desk, never available to explain what she wants done and when. She's always out and about, mixing at Rotary, mingling at Kiwanis. She is convinced that the fabric of life is woven by partnering, collaborating, networking, and liaisoning. She burns a lot of daylight developing theories, guidelines, and procedural manuals. She's high octane and she may be right.

Maybe I should follow her lead, start capitalizing words that are IMPORTANT, get certified, validated, and accredited, morph into an Answer Grape. Maybe I could become a Life Coach, spam the world with advice, and charge big bucks for little visits to discuss how to improve performance, productivity, and public image. I could help people organize their closets, garages, and desks. I could mentor career choices, transitions, and retirement. I could tell you why you hate your mother, whether to leave the Old Man, and how to get even with the next-door neighbor. What I don't know I can make up.

My friend Evelyn sports a diploma from a coach training school requiring hundreds of hours and thousands of dollars to provide access to essential tools and materials, discerning websites and newsletters, invaluable teleclasses and seminars. Before her husband left her (divorced her or just up and disappeared), Evelyn had an elegant uptown dress shop and became proficient at telling customers how swell they looked in mauve, while the dressing room mirror clearly indicated she was not altogether truthful. I could do that.

Or I could become an Image Consultant. I know what to wear to weddings, funerals, and tea at the Brown Palace Hotel, and more importantly, whether to go in the first place. I have enough self-esteem, self-confidence, and unmitigated gall to convince people that they can pursue and achieve personal and professional goals. I'm ready to substitute for parents, educators, clerics, and the lady next door. I can fill the void left by family and friends, who are desperately tired of suggesting that you read a good book, alter your attitude, get a haircut and a life.

Let's face it, there isn't an image in town that can't be improved by a day at the spa, a Chinese cooking class, or a hike up a four-teener. How hard can Life Coaching and Image Consulting be?

Gert-the-Extension-Agent

OLD GERT down at the Cooperative Extension Service knows it all. She *is* the Answer Grape. She knows how to upholster furniture, cook with lard, and get rid of skunk odor. She knows which canned fruit to put on top of vanilla pudding and which canned soup to put on top of noodles. She knows how to calibrate a weed sprayer and how to get rid of box elder bugs. She knows what to do with beets and how to bake at 12,000 feet.

Gert is a Family Resource Management Specialist. She has graduate degrees in crops and gardens, drought and fire, food and nutrition, wildlife and insects, soil and water, farm and home management. She is a resource's resource. She majored in ornamental grasses. So what if she's eighty years old and eighty pounds overweight? She knows how far to cut back Russian sage, how to make stuffing from stale bread, and how to get rid of spiders in the basement. So what if American agriculture has moved on?

In her day, Gert has given some spectacular workshops on how to make lye soap, whether potato salad should be served hot or cold, and what condiments to serve with ham hocks. Her seminar "Who Gets Grandma's Yellow Pie Plate?" shares more than you want to know about how to avoid family conflict when Granny bites the dust.

Gert is right there if you're cooking with kale, making rutabaga soufflé, sewing chintz curtains, or building an ant farm. But Gert hasn't been over the Pass in a few weeks. She still thinks a website is something spiders make in the corner of the closet.

She's just a newsletter away if you need to know when to get a soils test, how to use mulch, and whether prairie dogs can be poisoned. She knows age-appropriate chores for children, how to write out a shopping list, and when to freeze leftovers. It's scary how many tips she can share, even if her advice is, more often than not, "Take a deep breath and count the positives in your life—family, friends, health, skills, and interests—because just being alive is worth celebrating."

Gert may be the first person you turn to with a question about when to plant zinnias, but the last you'd call in the event of an attack by bioterrorists. She doesn't have a clue how to deal with plague, botulism, or smallpox. She is not equipped to help you decide whether or not to participate in a land conservation trust.

Gert's convinced that you can solve any problem—land management, water regulation, pollution control, or wildlife conservation—by hosting a coffee, holding a bake sale, or taking an environmentalist out to lunch.

The Boys at the Bar know different.

Someone at CSU told the state's 201.4 county agents and their 158.5 support staff that you can save agriculture, the environment, human health, and communities with a Power Point presentation. So all over America, farmers and ranchers are gathered about circular tables, munching on cookies provided by the Farm Bureau, and scribbling goals and objectives on Post-its and flip charts.

Down at Ph.D. school they assure you that things are more important if you write them in capital letters, that someone reads all those evaluation forms, and that the county commissioners give a rat's ass. They talk about alternatives and consequences instead of pros and cons, about being pro-active instead of reactive, about ongoing processes instead of tomorrow.

Problem is, Gert is talking to a room full of ranchers who hold degrees in agri-economics, fly airplanes, and use the Internet to buy and sell hay and cattle. Unlike Gert, they go over the Pass pretty regular. Gert's giving workshops on how to plan low-cost holiday dinners and these guys are wintering in Cancun. Gert's still fighting leafy spurge and the Boys at the Bar have been to China with economic development commissions exploring new markets for grain.

So next budget hearing, you might want to think about whether the county should be paying Gertie thirty grand a year to show old ladies how to make light fixtures out of Mason jars. The Boys at the Bar say they don't need a government-funded program to keep posted on which fruits prevent Jell-O from congealing. Mother Teresa didn't use a Palm Pilot so they sure-as-hell don't need them.

Mindi-the-Homeless-Rich-Homeowner

MY FRIEND MINDI is a baby boomer. She has a home in Boston, surrounded by universities that take pride in hosting more lectures, plays, and art exhibits than anyone can possibly attend, especially if they're schlepping kids to soccer and the dog to obedience school.

So why, I ask myself, does Mindi need a summer home on Whidbey Island, a cottage in New Hampshire, and a pied-à-terre in San Miguelle de Allende? How does she remember where she left the nutmeg, or the book she's reading? How does she find time to visit her significant other, who has a home in San Francisco and a condo at Snowmass? How many Day-Timers are required to track the landscapers, house nannies, and pool men? How much underwear does it take to accommodate life in five states and one foreign country?

Home-hopping involves a lot of windshield time, hours that might better be spent volunteering at the arts center. Keeping track of keys, electric bills, and vitamins requires a lot of energy, effort that could be devoted to helping out at a homeless shelter. Mindi doesn't drink at the Corral Club, eat lunch at the senior center, or belong to a book club. People who live on cul-de-sacs don't throw block parties. They want "community made easy," served up like a good tiramisu.

But community ain't easy. It was tough chasing the Indians out, bringing the railroad in, and building a ski area. Our new neighbors, like Mindi, are rich and beautiful. Dad is the CEO of a megabig cyber-corporation, and the lady of the house, the second or third wife, has nothing to do but attend yoga classes and remodel the kitchen. The house is bigger than the community center and the dog is walked in a fenced backyard on a leash.

According to a 2003 National Study of Second-Home Owners published in *American Demographics*, there are six million Mindi's in the world. Some days I'm convinced every one of them has moved into my town. The Eco-devos call them "economic drivers." They are driving up the cost of housing, food, and services. They are inflating demands for affordable housing, impacting natural resources, and increasing sprawl. Main Street merchants see them as profits, bureaucrats see them as tax dollars, and contractors see them as raw meat.

The Boys at the Bar called them turkeys in the '70s and still do. Demographers identify them as baby boomers. I call them depressing. They make me feel tired and poor. While they sip Starbucks and discuss focal points with interior decorators, I work three jobs. They cater sit-down dinners for their new friends, all gardeners, ski instructors, hairdressers, and people on their payrolls. I gas an '84 Subaru with tips from waiting tables. I hike wilderness roads to secret fishing holes, while they hire Orvis guides to take them to stocked ponds.

The homeless rich don't bake brownies for Little League, hold yard sales, or enter jams at the county fair. They can't name the county commissioners and they don't serve on school boards. They think Boone & Crockett were scouts for Lewis and Clark. They don't close fences and are amazed when bears play in their trash.

As the town grows bigger to accommodate their need to landscape forests and shop in boutiques, my world grows smaller. I have to go to the grocery store at six in the morning to avoid looking at women wearing lipstick. Some days I just want to sit in the hot tub down at the city pool and tell stories about whiteouts, suicides, droughts, bankruptcies, and the planning commission.

Colorado is blessed with twenty-four scenic and historic byways, thirteen national forests and grasslands, and eight national parks and monuments. Mindi wants to conquer them all, suck up mountain air, and splash in pristine streams. She doesn't give a rip about community consensus, mitigating impacts, our history, lifestyle, and culture. She is not interested in discussing community amenities, affordable housing, quality of life, ranchland conservation, economic indicators, park and trail systems, or cultural amenities. She just wants them up and running when her plane lands.

Every survey we do—and the town hires fancy-pants, out-of-state consultants to conduct 'em every hour on the hour—concludes that we are unique because we are *nice*. The polls all say the same thing, always have. Ask me one more time and I might not be so bloody nice. Nice didn't work for the Indians and it's not going to contain the second-home owner tsunami.

Wanda-Jane-the-Hellion

THERE'S SOMETHING ABOUT Wyoming people that has always made me nervous: something in the air or water that compels them to steal trash cans and shoot out road signs, get 86'd from bars, leave ridiculous messages on answering machines, dance on tables at the Dixon Club, and go on runners.

Wanda Jane Lockhart was born and raised in Baggs, Wyoming, twenty-one miles north of the last gas station in America. She was a Boone & Crockett–sized playmate—trouble looking for a homestead. We were neighbors and she made me nervous for thirty years.

She wore mismatched socks in size five red boots, and 28-31 Wranglers, which accounted for the fact that no one had ever seen her legs. She had shoe-polish-black cropped hair and a wrinkled grin, the kind that suggested she had just stuffed fresh roadkill into a coffee can and sent it to her sister-in-law. Wanda Jane hated her sister-in-law, enough to make a life-sized doll that hung in effigy or was displayed in compromising positions on her front porch.

Wanda Jane spent a third of her sixty years delivering mail on unpaved roads from Steamboat Springs to Twenty Mile Park, Cow Creek, Hilton Gulch, Pleasant Valley, Yellow Jacket Pass, and Strawberry Park. Her red Australian shepherd shared the front seat on the sixty-eight-mile daily trek, and through the years, she clocked enough miles to go to the moon and back. She said she killed three Jeep Cherokees, and the fourth, the only one she bought new, died with its tires up.

Wanda Jane was the only rural route carrier with "FEMAIL" on her license plate. She boasted that she never had a sick day and never suffered from anything more than a hangover, which, she insisted, didn't count. She delivered *Fencepost* magazines to fifth-generation cattlemen in weathered ranch houses and *Wall Street Journals* to Cappuccino Cowboys in trophy homes she called "three-holers." She delivered birth and death notices to her boxholders, and they left her homemade cinnamon rolls.

Her mail aerobics began at dawn, and if she didn't break down or spend too much time chatting, ended with a burger and beer at the Corral Club. Wanda Jane and the local pub were pieced from the same fabric, stuff the chamber of commerce doesn't regard as essential to "economic development."

Wanda Jane drank Budweiser, cans for every day and long necks for fancy, and presided over the table near the back door. It was a round, Algonquin-style table, headquarters for Stomps and Freaks and the I Don't Give a Shit Club of which Wanda Jane was president. The club never held a meeting because no one gave a shit. The Corral Club is where Wanda Jane found smiles while she raised four children, and her husband took bareback championships on the rodeo circuit. That's where she told stories about the time she peed in the whiskey bottle to stop the hired man from nipping, stole an outhouse so the class of '77 could float in the river race, and got herself invited to dinner with sheepherders up in Whiskey Park.

The world was a kinder, simpler place when Wanda Jane was roasting stolen chickens under the bridge at Fortification Creek, telling stories and lies and not much caring which was which. She had more'n her share of fun before Uncle Irlan, loan officer at the local bank, took her car keys away.

Last year was a tough time for postal patrons on Rural Route 1. Their Mail Lady lost a battle with cancer. The Corral Club was sold to a lady from the East who won the lottery, cleaned the grease trap, and began serving really bad Tex-Mex. A fitness center and tanning salon opened in the vacant co-op building and, over at the chamber of commerce, they began holding focus groups to decide not how many stoplights the town should have but how many "pillows" the lodging community would provide. Like the Boys at the Bar, Wanda Jane would think it far too many.

About the Author

SUREVA TOWLER lectures on how to write local history and has written award-winning histories of Northwest Colorado. She is active in the Colorado Author's League and Western Writers of America, and her essays about how people and communities adapt to change appear regularly in the *Denver Post*. She lives in Steamboat Springs, Colorado.